W9-CPE-327

WITHDRAWN

# Bioethics
## *Who Lives, Who Dies, and Who Decides?*

ISSUES IN FOCUS TODAY

Linda Jacobs Altman

**Enslow Publishers, Inc.**
40 Industrial Road
Box 398
Berkeley Heights, NJ  07922
USA

http://www.enslow.com

Library of Congress Cataloging-in-Publication Data

Altman, Linda Jacobs, 1943–
      Bioethics : who lives, who dies, and who decides? / Linda Jacobs Altman.
         p. cm. — (Issues in focus today)
      Includes bibliographical references and index.
      ISBN-10: 0-7660-2546-2
      1. Medical ethics—Juvenile literature. 2. Bioethics—Juvenile literature.
   I. Title. II. Series.
      R724.A584 2006
      174'.957—dc22

                                                          2006007002

ISBN-13: 978-0-7660-2546-2

Printed in the United States of America

10 9 8 7 6 5 4 3 2

To Our Readers:
We have done our best to make sure that all Internet Addresses in this book were active
and appropriate when we went to press. However, the author and publisher have no
control over and assume no liability for the material available on those Internet sites
or on other Web sites they may link to. Any comments or suggestions can be sent by
e-mail to comments@enslow.com or to the address on the back cover.

Illustration Credits: Agricultural Research Service/USDA, p. 39; AP/Wide World, pp. 74,
78, 91, 103, 105; Digital Stock, p. 35; Getty Images, pp. 42, 101; Photo Researchers, pp. 1,
3, 10, 20, 46, 49, 60, 66, 69, 81, 85, 88, 96; Photos.com, pp. 5, 16, 31; RubberBall
Productions, pp. 26, 53, 56, 64, 99; U.S. Centers for Disease Control and Prevention,
pp. 3, 28.

Cover Illustrations: Shutterstock (large photo); BananaStock (small photo).

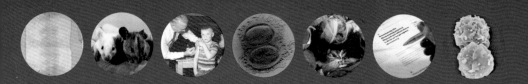

# C o n t e n t s

# The Biotech Revolution

On April 14, 2003, scientists gathered in Bethesda, Maryland, to celebrate a historic breakthrough. After thirteen long years, the Human Genome Project had sequenced, or mapped, the genetic code—the biochemical structure of human heredity.

The end of the project signaled the beginning of a new era: the genomic age. Many believe that this genomic age will define the twenty-first century as the atomic age defined the twentieth.

At the dawning of this genomic age, three interrelated disciplines have come into their own: genetics, biotechnology, and bioethics. Genetics deals with the mechanisms of heredity—how traits are transmitted from one generation to the next.

Biotechnology is applied science, developing ways to put this knowledge to use. Finally, bioethics focuses on the personal, social, and moral consequences of scientific and medical advances.

## A Short History of Bioethics

The word *bioethics* did not exist until 1970, when Dr. Van Rensselaer Potter coined it to describe "biology combined with diverse humanistic knowledge [medicine, law, politics, philosophy], forging a science that sets a system of medical and environmental priorities for acceptable survival."[1]

By the early 1980s, bioethics was becoming an academic discipline in its own right. Colleges and universities offered courses and even degrees in bioethics. Professional organizations developed guidelines for ethical behavior in medicine and scientific research.

Bioethics extended and included medical ethics, which dates back to the Greek physician Hippocrates, some five hundred years B.C. His guidelines for the doctor-patient relationship set down basic principles that are still in use today. For example, the idea that a doctor "should never do harm to anyone" came from the Hippocratic oath.[2] So did the concept of what is now called patient confidentiality: "All that may come to my knowledge in the exercise of my profession . . . which ought not to be spread abroad, I will keep secret and will never reveal."[3]

The Hippocratic oath applies to doctor-patient relationships. Other ethical statements focus on the rights of human subjects in biomedical experiments. Other codes have focused on the rights of human subjects in laboratory testing. Probably the best known of these statements is the Nuremberg Code of 1947. It took shape after World War II, when war crimes trials revealed that Nazi doctors and scientists had performed inhuman and unnecessary experiments on concentration camp prisoners.

The ten-point code begins with a statement that "the voluntary consent of the human subject is absolutely essential" to participation in any study.[4] Other clauses relate to the safety of the subjects and the obligation to terminate any experiment that proves to be hazardous to them.

Seventeen years later, the World Medical Association created the Declaration of Helsinki, which broadened and clarified the major principles of the Nuremberg Code. While the general principles of Helsinki and Nuremberg are still relevant in the twenty-first century, advances in genetics have raised a whole new group of ethical questions. Scientists and ethicists sometimes find themselves at a loss to answer those questions without provoking bitter, and even violent, disagreement.

## An Adventure Into Ourselves

The Human Genome Project itself became an ethical issue for some people. Those who worried that scientists were delving into matters best left to God called the project dangerous, maybe even evil. Dr. Francis S. Collins of the National Human Genome Research Institute called it "an amazing adventure into ourselves," which would allow scientists "to understand our own DNA instruction book, the shared inheritance of all humankind."[5]

This exploration was a shared effort. From its beginning in 1990, the Human Genome Project was multinational: China, France, Germany, Great Britain, Japan, and the United States all participated. Hundreds of scientists worked at twenty centers around the world, each group concentrating on a different part of the task.

In May 1998, biologist J. Craig Venter announced that he had formed a company called Celera Genomics. According to Venter, Celera would sequence the entire human genome by 2001, four years ahead of HGP's projected conclusion. This triggered a competition between the two groups.

The HGP teams pushed themselves and completed the work more than two years ahead of schedule. In April 2003, both HGP and Celera announced that they had succeeded in mapping the human genome. According to a news release from the National Human Genome Research Institute, "Having the essentially complete sequence of the human genome is similar to having all the pages of a manual needed to make the human body."[6]

The HGP made the completed work freely available on the Internet. Science has rarely seen this kind of openness and cooperation. Research is traditionally competitive—a struggle to be first to find the equation, crack the code, solve the mystery.

In this world of hard facts, ethical and social concerns have often fallen by the wayside. Critics accuse scientists of focusing on what *can* be done, not what *should* be done. According to journalist and environmentalist Bill McKibben, "Some people assume the very debate [over technological issues] is irrelevant—[They] assume that we will inevitably develop . . . new technologies to the fullest [no matter] what anyone says."[7]

These assumptions can be dangerous, since scientific advances already seem to be coming faster than humanity's ability to cope with them. Runaway technology could lead individuals and societies down roads they would rather not travel.

## Science and Ethics: A Brand New Day

The designers of the Human Genome Project did not just give lip service to curbing runaway technology in the name of ethics. They set aside three percent of HGP's budget to fund ELSI: the study of Ethical, Legal, and Social Issues connected with decoding the blueprint for human life. It was the first time that ethical considerations had been specifically funded as part of a scientific research project.

Biologist James Watson, winner of the Nobel prize, played a

major role in forming and funding ELSI. In 1953, Watson and his partner Francis Crick discovered the structure of DNA (deoxyribonucleic acid), the famous double helix structure that carries the code for creating a living organism.

Watson knew that decoding that information could give humankind once-unthinkable control over its own evolution. In the process, it would challenge long-held beliefs and force people to look at old issues in new ways.

Watson believed that preparing for the practical and ethical issues was as important as doing the research itself. Would people begin enhancing the genetic structure of their offspring? Would there be new forms of discrimination based on genetics? Would societies use genetics to breed people who could be easily controlled? Watson wanted ELSI to provide genetic education, teaching people how to confront such questions and make intelligent choices.

## Studying the Mechanisms of Heredity

In the mid-1800s, people realized that an organism inherits traits from its parents; however, they did not know how traits passed from one generation to the next. An Austrian monk named Gregor Mendel decided to find out about heredity.

He studied common garden peas, focusing on seven specific traits: seed color, seed shape, flower color, stem length, shape when ripe, color of unripe pods, and position of flowers on the stem. Each trait had only two ways of being expressed. For example, seed color could be yellow or green; seed shape, smooth or wrinkled.

Mendel knew that some kind of biochemical structures passed traits from one generation to the next. He called these structures *factors*. Today, they are called *genes*.

Genes exist within the nucleus, or core, of an organism's cells. They are positioned on rodlike structures called chromosomes. All organisms get half their genes from each parent. The

James Watson (on left) and Francis Crick pose with their model of the DNA molecule in 1953. Their discovery of the structure of DNA, which carries the code for every living organism, revolutionized science.

DNA inside those genes carries the code of life. DNA resembles a rope ladder, with "rungs" made of substances called *nucleotides*. They form a kind of chemical alphabet with just four letters: A, C, T, and G (for the biochemicals adenine, cytosine, thymine, and guanine). These letters work together in what are known as base pairs: A with T and C with G.

The human genome has about three billion base pairs, an incredibly long sequence of As and Ts, Cs and Gs, interacting to create a new individual. If all the letters in a single genome were printed out, the code would fill a stack of books as high as the Washington Monument (more than 555 feet).[8]

There is little room for error in the code. Even small misspellings can have disastrous results. For example, three missing letters on Chromosome 7 account for cystic fibrosis (CF). CF is a disease in which the lungs and other organs fill with thick mucus. Until recently, victims did not live through childhood. Improved treatment has extended the life span into the thirties for some people, but there is no actual cure. Many scientists claim that gene therapy will one day produce that cure.

## Gene Therapy: Beginnings

Gene therapy involves replacing defective genes with healthy ones that have been carefully engineered, or altered, for the purpose. The beginnings of gene therapy have been beset with conflicts between those who believe it will eventually produce medical miracles and those who worry that the risk may be too great. Early cases have given ammunition to both sides of the argument.

In 1990, a team of researchers used gene therapy to treat adenosine deaminase (ADA) deficiency. ADA deficiency is a disorder of the immune system in which one faulty gene prevents the body from manufacturing the enzyme ADA. Lack of ADA causes the immune system to shut down, leaving victims at the mercy of every germ that comes along. With neither a cure nor an effective treatment, few ADA children lived long enough to go to kindergarten. Fewer still reach their teens.

Doctors Kenneth Culver, R. Michael Blaese, and W. French Anderson set out to change that. They began experimenting on mice and other animals, looking for a way to replace faulty genes with healthy ones.

The word *bioethics* did not even exist until 1970. But by the early 1980s, bioethics was becoming an academic discipline in its own right.

Under ordinary circumstances, it would have been years before anybody tried this technique on human beings. However, Ashanthi De Silva and Cynthia Cutshall could not wait for years. Ashanthi was four years old; Cynthia, nine. Both of them had ADA deficiency, and both of them were running out of time.

In spite of the incomplete laboratory data, the doctors wanted to use gene replacement therapy on the girls. It was a desperate gamble in desperate circumstances. The ethics committees of the National Institutes of Health and the Food and Drug Administration approved the procedure. Both sets of parents agreed.

With everything in place, the doctors set to work. They started with Ashanthi because she was the sickest of the two girls. Their chief problem was finding a way to deliver the healthy genes to the proper site in the girls' bodies. Ordinary injections proved worthless; ADA genes could not survive in the bloodstream. Then the doctors decided to try a virus.

It seemed a perfect choice. Viruses cannot reproduce themselves. They survive by invading cells and forcing them to make copies of the virus. This destroys the cell, which ruptures and releases its contents into the body.

The researchers decided to use viruses as a delivery system by replacing their normal content with healthy ADA genes.

The modified viruses delivered the genes to the proper place, and the treatment worked.

Not only did the girls have fewer infections, they became more energetic. After a year of treatment, both were attending public schools, taking part in activities, and generally living normal lives. The doctors stress that Cynthia and Ashanthi are not cured. Both require medications and periodic booster treatments with healthy ADA genes. Still, these two pioneering patients count as a success story in the field of genetic engineering.

## The Death of Jesse Gelsinger

If Cynthia and Ashanthi represent glowing success for gene therapy, eighteen-year-old Jesse Gelsinger represents just the opposite—the high costs of taking risks with new and untried genetic treatments. The Arizona teenager was born with a rare disorder called ornithine transcarbamylase deficiency, or OTC.

In OTC, a missing gene interferes with the liver's ability to metabolize, or break down, ammonia. This allows toxic, or poisonous, levels of ammonia to build up in the liver. Babies born with the most severe form of OTC usually die within weeks of birth. Survivors rarely live to see their fifth birthday.

With a milder form of OTC, Jesse Gelsinger led a relatively normal life, though he had to take 32 pills a day and follow a special low-protein diet. Jesse's condition was not immediately life-threatening, and he qualified for a study of a new treatment that was being tested.

On September 13, 1999, Jesse received an injection of a virus that had been genetically altered to carry the missing gene. The next day, he developed jaundice (yellow skin), which indicates a liver malfunction. He sank into a coma and never revived. On September 17, Jesse Gelsinger died.

Jesse's case raised both scientific and ethical questions. The risk to Ashanthi De Silva and Cynthia Cutshall was tremendous, but both girls were out of options. Gene therapy offered the only chance to save their lives. In the minds of the doctors and the girls' parents, this fact justified a high degree of risk.

The situation was different for Jesse Gelsinger; his life was not in immediate danger. He volunteered for a university study to help increase medical knowledge about his disorder. His death raised many questions: Were the possible benefits worth the risk to Jesse and other study participants? Did the researchers have enough solid laboratory data to justify human experimentation? Did they select and monitor the test subjects carefully enough? Did Jesse fully understand the possible complications and consequences?

There are no hard-and-fast answers to questions such as these; reasonable people can and do disagree. For example, researchers might disagree about the risk-to-benefit ratio of a planned study; they might have different standards about what is enough laboratory data to justify human experimentation.

## Coming to Terms with Science and Change

Many skeptics base their opinions of genetics on some version of the "slippery slope." The basic idea behind this argument is that a first step in any given direction makes it easier to take the next, and the next, going down the slope to a terrible result.

For example, the slippery slope is a common argument against assisted suicide for the terminally ill. If doctors could help dying patients kill themselves, the next step might be helping the chronically ill or the severely disabled to die, then anybody who considers life a burden. And so it would go, until suicide becomes socially acceptable and cheapens the value of human life.

Scientific ideas have often triggered controversy. In the early nineteenth century, Charles Darwin dared to say that life—human life included—evolved from simple, one-celled organisms. He was condemned, ridiculed, and ostracized, or excluded, because his theory of evolution challenged religious doctrines of creation.

Darwin's theory placed humankind on the evolutionary "ladder." Thus, humans might be the most advanced and intelligent of animals, but they were animals nonetheless. They shared the biological heritage of all other living creatures.

As humankind takes control of its own biological destiny, medical science will develop an impressive array of uses—everything from repairing genetic flaws and curing once-incurable diseases to identifying criminals from their DNA and extending the human life span. How people deal with these advances will not only shape science and medicine, but determine what it means to be human in the genomic age.

# Research and Development

Supposedly, pure science does not deal in opinion, philosophy, or belief. It deals in facts that can be proved and experiments that can be repeated over and over again, always with the same result.

Those facts are presumably value-neutral; neither good nor bad, right nor wrong. A flawed gene is abnormal, not unethical. Bacteria and viruses are not evil because they produce disease. Ethics involves choice, and neither genes nor germs can choose their own behavior. Only human beings can do that.

## Ethics and Risk-Taking

In science, making choices often means taking chances. Risk is generally considered a necessary and accepted part of the process. To the extent that this is true, the most that scientists can do is take sensible precautions. They can contain hazardous materials so they do not escape into the environment. They can protect human experimental subjects from harm and provide for the humane care of laboratory animals.

Even with protective measures in place, biomedical research can involve some hard choices. So can medical treatment, especially with newer, cutting-edge drugs or procedures. For example, suppose a new drug could destroy cancer cells, but would subject the patient to dangerous, even deadly, side effects (unintended results of taking the drug or having the procedure). Is treatment worth the risk on the outside chance of a cure?

There is no one-size-fits-all answer to such questions. However, there is a guideline: the idea of acceptable risk. It varies from one case to another.

Acceptable risk for a generally healthy thirty-year-old would not be the same as that for a sixty-year-old with high blood pressure. What might be considered unthinkable risk for the older patient could be entirely acceptable for the younger one. Another factor is the severity of the patient's condition. If the patient will surely die without treatment, then greater risk is warranted regardless of his or her age.

Sometimes, patients will define acceptable risk for themselves. This is especially true for people with disabling chronic conditions or terminal illnesses. They may volunteer for high-risk studies or treatments with new drugs or procedures.

For example, Deneane Chiplock of Saginaw, Michigan, known as Dee, belonged to a family with a long history of amyotrophic lateral sclerosis. ALS, as it is commonly called, is a fatal neurological disease. It gradually paralyzes the victim until he or she cannot move, talk, or even breathe.

When ALS struck Dee Chiplock in November 2003, she had already watched her mother, two aunts, two great-aunts, and grandfather die of the disease. They had seemed resigned to their fate. Chiplock wanted her life and her death to make a difference. She knew that she could not save her own life, but perhaps she could help to save others.

She became an activist for ALS, lobbying Congress for research funds, and volunteering to test a drug that had slowed the progress of ALS in laboratory animals. When doctors worried about the risks, Chiplock silenced them with one question: "Why not experiment with me since I'm dying anyway?"[1]

Faced with this determined and well-informed patient, doctors and researchers agreed to the trial. The drug may have slowed Chiplock's deterioration, but not by much. Dee Chiplock died on May 4, 2005, eighteen months after her diagnosis. She was forty years old.

## Tests on Animals

Under present-day medical research codes, researchers cannot subject human beings to unusual dangers. They certainly cannot design experiments that will lead to the death of human subjects.

There are no such constraints with animals. There are guidelines for the humane treatment of laboratory animals—for example, the American Psychological Association's Committee on Animal Research and Ethics says that psychologists should act on the assumption that procedures that would produce pain in humans will also do so in other animals. However, the guidelines do not forbid causing pain or conducting experiments that will kill the animal subject.

For most of history, animals have been considered natural resources, to be used as humans saw fit. Their lives were not seen as having value in and of themselves.

The ancient Greeks practiced vivisection, or dissection of a living animal. With no anesthetics at their disposal, the Greek researchers cut up animals that were fully awake. If they had any ethical qualms about this practice, they left no record of them.

Not until the nineteenth century did the plight of laboratory animals become an ethical issue. In 1875, Frances Power Cobbe of London, England founded the world's first antivivisection group: the Society for the Protection of Animals Liable to Vivisection. By the next year, the society's activities had helped to produce England's first Cruelty to Animals Act.

Exactly one hundred years later in the United States, Australian philosopher Peter Singer published a book called *Animal Liberation*. It was 1975,

**Ethics involves choice, and neither genes nor germs can choose their own behavior. Only human beings can do that.**

a time when eager social reformers wanted to make a difference. They stood against racism, sexism, materialism, and exploitation in all its forms.

Many of them became interested in the use of animal subjects for scientific experiments. In 1980, the more radical of these activists formed People for the Ethical Treatment of Animals (PETA).

The new organization began with a mission statement that made its position clear: "PETA operates under the simple principle that animals are not ours to eat, wear, experiment on, or use for entertainment."[2] Animals, according to PETA, have a right to be treated with respect and compassion. Their lives have value in themselves and should not be thrown away like so many disposable dust cloths. PETA opposes scientific testing on animals, under any circumstances and for any reason. It is known for high-visibility protest demonstrations and for an unwillingness to compromise on what it considers immoral behavior.

The Humane Society of the United States (HSUS) also wants to end animal testing, but its approach is generally more restrained than PETA's. The HSUS promotes alternative testing

Two mice sit on a researcher's hand. Though there are some guidelines as to how laboratory animals should be treated, they do not forbid causing pain or even death to the animal.

methods with its *Three Rs* program: replacement, reduction, and refinement.

Thus, workable alternatives to animal testing would include the following: completely *replacing* animal tests with other methods whenever and wherever possible, *reducing* the number of animals used in experiments, and *refining*, or improving, testing procedures to reduce animal stress and pain as much as possible.

Scientists and others who defend animal research do not go so far as to say that the suffering and pain of an animal does not matter. Most call for good animal care and test procedures that are as humane as possible. However, they do not see animal experimentation as an ethical issue.

In an article on animal protectionism, Patrick H. Cleveland of the Coalition For Animals and Animal Research (CFAAR) focused on the benefits of animal research. He said that animal protectionists

> do a great disservice to patients suffering from the hundreds of diseases we are still trying to cure. Those patients are important— more important than animals. There is a fundamental difference between respect and consideration for animals . . . and granting them equal moral rights, just as there is a fundamental difference between humans and animals.[3]

## Clinical Trials

Those who stress the importance of animal testing sometimes point out that animal experiments allow them to fine-tune a new drug or procedure before trying it on human subjects in studies known as clinical trials.

There are four phases in most clinical trials. In Phase I, researchers test a small group of volunteers. Most often, the study will be done in a clinic setting, so the subjects are close to medical aid in case of trouble. Dose-ranging studies establish how much of the new medication is necessary to produce the desired result without serious side effects. Phase II studies involve a larger group of subjects. The researchers concentrate on how well the drug works for its intended purpose and look for toxic, or poisonous, effects.

After a successful Phase II, the drug is ready for large-scale testing. In Phase III, the double-blind study is the most common experimental design. To prevent unintentional bias, researchers divide the test subjects into experimental and control groups. The experimental group receives the drug under investigation. The control group receives a placebo, or sugar pill. Neither the subjects nor those conducting the experiment know which group is which until the study is completed.

Finally, Phase IV trials check drug safety issues. Researchers look for side effects. The researchers are ethically obligated to reveal any potential problems.

Minor side effects should be mentioned in patient instructions. Major ones may call for restricting use to certain, well-defined situations. If a side effect can cause serious or permanent damage, the drug may have to be abandoned despite the millions of dollars and worker hours invested in its development.

With so much at stake, some people may be tempted to understate the dangers or overstate the benefits of a drug or treatment. That would be illegal as well as unethical. In spite of this, some researchers have succumbed to temptation and used deceit to save their work.

## Research Abuses

Sooner or later, most discussions of ethics and human research will come around to the horrifying experiments in World War II Germany. Nazi doctors experimented on concentration camp prisoners. They immersed prisoners in freezing water to see how long they would survive, injected them with live pathogens, or germs, and performed surgeries without anesthetic. Many other experiments were just as horrifying. The Nazis called this "science."

Others called it murder. After the war, twenty-three Nazi doctors stood trial in Nuremberg, Germany, for their crimes. The tribunal sentenced seven of these doctors to death, found five not guilty, and gave the rest sentences ranging from ten years to life in prison.

These were the horrors that prompted the tribunal to create the Nuremberg Code. Medical societies all over the world soon accepted its principles. Unfortunately, that acceptance did not put an end to abuses. Unethical practices have not been limited to dictatorships and countries with poor human rights records. They have occurred in prosperous Western democracies, including the United States.

## The Tuskegee Study

In 1932, the United States Public Health Service sponsored a study of untreated syphilis among African-American men. The Tuskegee Institute, an all-black college in Alabama, administered the program. All the subjects in the Tuskegee study lived in Macon County, Alabama, where the disease had reached epidemic proportions. The African-American community was hardest hit, with 35 to 40 percent of its population infected.

Participants came from among the poorest sharecroppers in the county. Some were illiterate; many had never been examined by a doctor. The research team did not mention the word "syphilis." They said that the men had "bad blood" and offered to treat it. Participants would receive regular medical care, free meals, and burial insurance. All they had to do was allow researchers to examine them from time to time.

In fact, the researchers had no intention of treating the men; just the opposite. They wanted to find out how the disease would progress with no treatment at all. At the time, there was no cure for syphilis. Existing treatments were so ineffective that the researchers suspected patients would do as well without them.

Six hundred men agreed to participate: 399 with syphilis and a control group of 201 who did not have the disease. The study was supposed to last six months. It would continue for forty years.

In the beginning, there seemed to be no harm in continuing to follow these men. Then penicillin came on the scene, and was soon recognized as a complete cure for syphilis. In 1947, the Public Health Service ran clinics all over the country, giving free penicillin injections to all comers.

The Tuskegee researchers deliberately withheld treatment from their subjects. They continued their study with a new goal: to find out how untreated syphilis spreads and kills.

They made plans for detailed autopsies, or after-death examinations. Then they watched as the disease took its toll on the men in the study. Vital organs malfunctioned. Some of the victims went blind. Some developed dementia as memory and reasoning power failed them. When someone died, the researchers examined the body. Then the free burial insurance paid funeral expenses.

The Tuskegee study continued until 1972, when Associated Press reporter Jean Heller broke the story. On July 25, the *Washington Evening Star* gave it a front page headline: "Syphilis Patients Died Untreated."[4] The next morning, newspapers all over the country carried the story.

By that time, 128 men had died of syphilis or its complications. Forty wives had become infected, and nineteen babies were born with the disease.[5]

Amid an outburst of public indignation, the government shut down the study. "Tuskegee" became a watchword for unethical research.

## The Willowbrook Study

A study at the Willowbrook State Institution in New York went beyond withholding treatment. Researchers deliberately infected their subjects with hepatitis B, an incurable disease that damages the liver.

Most of the subjects in the study had severe mental retardation. They could not speak for themselves. Hector DeJesus was an exception. He came to Willowbrook in the early 1960s, as a "hyperactive and unmanageable" child from an abusive home.

Nearly forty years later, DeJesus learned that he had been a human guinea pig for secret medical experiments. Investigative reporter Sarah Wallace broke the story on the WABC evening news for February 1, 2005. Beginning in 1956 and continuing until 1971, a group of Willowbrook doctors had purposely infected disabled children with hepatitis B.

DeJesus knew at once that he had been part of that experiment, and he knew that he had to speak out about what happened. He took his story to WABC, where he talked at length with Sarah Wallace.

He remembered being moved into the medical building. He had no idea why, because he was not sick; none of the children appeared to be, either. "It wasn't until I went to the medical building that I actually came down with hepatitis and got sick—very sick," DeJesus said. "I was near death. And there were people being taken to the morgue just about every day."[6]

Stories like this horrified the public. The perpetrators of the hepatitis B experiment were not Nazis experimenting on concentration camp prisoners. They were American doctors, members of a profession that was supposed to save lives, not put them at risk.

Dr. Michael Wilkins observed how these doctors behaved toward the children in their study: "The mentality was they [the subjects] don't feel discomfort, they don't feel illness." This allowed experimenters to justify "placing [the children] in some sort of subhuman category."[7]

This dehumanizing of test subjects is common in unethical studies. So is deception. For example, the Willowbrook researchers told families that their children would benefit from the study. They also claimed that children would not be admitted to the hospital unless they participated in the study.

This was a significant threat. By the time parents turned to Willowbrook, their children were usually too disruptive to keep at home. Regular schools and community-based programs could not cope with children who had severe mental retardation or behavioral problems. Faced with this dilemma and reassured that the study would benefit their children, many parents agreed.

According to Dr. David Rothman, "The word that runs through the consent form again and again is prevention. We are

Stringent rules govern the way scientific research is conducted today. However, abuses do occur, most commonly in research that poses a high level of risk to human subjects.

going to prevent this disease in your child. But of course, it was completely misleading. Deceitful."[8]

Overall, deception is actually rare, but it does occur, despite codes of conduct and the growth of bioethics as a profession. The practice of withholding important information is most common in studies that involve high risk to human subjects.

For example, the Willowbrook researchers knew that they could not recruit subjects by telling the truth about their study. What parent would allow a child to be infected with a deadly virus?

The researchers could have taken the ethical high ground by abandoning or revising the study. Instead, they deceived families about the true nature of their project.

Some even tried to rationalize their actions. For example, one doctor claimed that living conditions were so bad that the children would have gotten hepatitis anyway. The researchers were simply giving it to them earlier.[9]

Cases such as this do not inspire confidence. They stand out from the thousands of studies that are conducted according to the highest ethical and scientific standards. The public focuses on the Willowbrooks and Tuskegees and reacts with justifiable horror.

Ethical statements such as the Nuremberg Code and the Declaration of Helsinki cannot entirely eliminate abuses, nor can they eliminate disputes over what is, and what is not, ethical behavior. People of good will can disagree about how to define "acceptable risk."

As biotechnology produces new experimental drugs and procedures, the debate can be expected to grow. Some will embrace the brave new world of the genomic age; others will fear and resist it. Regardless of these conflicts and disagreements, the challenge remains the same: balancing scientific progress with human values and human rights.

Public Health: The Good of the Many

Some bioethical issues affect society as a whole, without necessarily touching every individual. For example, a wide-spread epidemic endangers everyone, not just those who get sick. When public health and safety are at stake, the guiding principle is the greatest good for the greatest number.

Public health agencies can quarantine, or segregate, sick people to keep infections from spreading. They can require vaccinations for students in public schools. The Food and Drug Administration (FDA) can enforce hygiene regulations on everything from fast food chains to five-star restaurants. It evaluates new drugs for safety and effectiveness; no drug can be sold without its approval.

Most people accept these programs. The minor interference with personal rights seems justified by the benefits to society. However, some programs meet unexpected resistance.

## The Fluoridation Wars

Some form of water treatment has existed since 4000 B.C. These early efforts were designed to improve taste and appearance. The ancients boiled water, filtered it through charcoal, and strained it.

It was not until the mid-nineteenth century that scientists became concerned about waterborne diseases. In 1855, London physician John Snow traced a deadly outbreak of cholera to contaminated water in a single well. At the time, no one knew how to decontaminate the water. The only option was to shut down the well.

By the early twentieth century, scientists learned that a chemical known as chlorine could kill pathogens in drinking water. Adding a small amount to the water killed cholera germs, as well as those that produced dysentery and typhoid.

Some forty-five years later, scientists discovered that another chemical, fluoride, could reduce tooth decay in children. The evidence was strong; the technology simple and inexpensive. By the mid-1950s, fluoridation of municipal water supplies had become commonplace in both the United States and Europe. It had also become controversial.

Some opponents called it dangerous, some called it useless, and some called it an inexcusable breach of ethics. The controversy has continued into the twenty-first century. For example, in 2005, a posting on one holistic healing Web site claimed: "Fluoridation amounts to forced medication of the water supply." Furthermore, according to the posting, it demonstrated "a complete lack of ethics on the part of its promoters."[1]

Supporters of fluoridation include the American Dental Association and the American Academy of Family Physicians

(AAFP). To them, adding fluoride is a simple public health measure; it is no different from adding chlorine to prevent waterborne diseases.

In a policy statement on the issue, the AAFP stated: "Fluoridation of public water supplies is a safe, economical, and effective measure to prevent dental [decay]." The policy statement also advised fluoride supplements for children from six months to sixteen years old when fluoride levels in drinking water are low.[2]

Despite all evidence to the contrary, opponents of fluoridation continue to deny its effectiveness and safety. They question the accuracy of study methods, claiming that fluoride actually harms teeth and bones.

Their strongest argument against fluoridation does not involve science at all; it involves ethics and civil liberties. Opponents claim that fluoridating public water supplies violates individual rights, forcing everyone to consume the fluoride whether they want to or not.

## Typhoid Mary

At the turn of the twentieth century, the case of Mary Mallon triggered a conflict between public health and individual rights. Mallon was an Irish immigrant who worked as a cook. She was also a carrier of typhoid fever, a serious bacterial disease that causes fever, weakness, and, in extreme cases, death. She had never had the disease, yet could infect others simply by handling their food.

The public saga of "Typhoid Mary" began in the summer of 1906. Mallon took a job cooking for a family in Oyster Bay, Long Island. Shortly after she started work, members of the household began getting sick; first one of the children, then two of the maids. Altogether, eleven members of the household came down with typhoid fever.

Just three weeks after it struck, Mary Mallon quit her job and disappeared. The owners of the house hired typhoid expert George Soper to investigate the outbreak. When he learned that the cook had quit suddenly, he sensed that it might be important.

Soper tracked Mallon's employment record. The evidence was clear: wherever she went, typhoid followed. To verify his suspicions, Sopher asked Mallon to submit blood and stool samples for testing. When she refused, public health officials in New York took her into custody. They performed the tests without her consent. As they had expected, Mallon carried the live typhoid bacillus.

She refused to believe this, arguing that she never in her life had typhoid. This even puzzled the experts until they realized

The American Dental Association supports fluoridation of the water supply, since it has been shown to reduce cavities. Opponents see it as a civil liberties issue, not just a health issue.

that Mary Mallon was a "healthy carrier." She would remain forever immune to the disease, yet forever toxic to others.

For lack of a better solution, the health department took her to a hospital on North Brother Island in New York City's East River. There she could be safely isolated. The doctors asked her to promise that she would never again work as a cook. Mallon refused. In her mind, that would be admitting that the doctors were right.

She stayed on North Brother Island until 1910, when a new health commissioner decided to free her. He asked her to promise that she would not work as a cook. This time, Mallon gave her word.

For five years, she kept it. Then in 1915, typhoid fever broke out at a maternity hospital. Twenty-five people came down with the disease; two of them died. Public health officials traced the outbreak to a new cook, known only as "Mrs. Brown." It was Mary Mallon, working under an assumed name.

The health department faced an ethical dilemma. They had to choose between placing the public in danger by releasing a known typhoid carrier, or violating Mallon's constitutional rights by imprisoning her though she had not broken any existing law.

With no workable alternative at hand, the department fell back upon a familiar principle: the greatest good for the greatest number. Mary Mallon went back to North Brother Island, where she remained until her death in November 1938.

Ethics is full of choices like this: complex cases in which the authorities cannot be entirely fair, because they must choose between the good of the one and the good of the many.

## AIDS and HIV

In the early 1980s, a new disease brought up the same old conflicts between individual rights and the public good. AIDS, or acquired immunodeficiency syndrome, destroys the body's ability to fight infection. Victims contract one infectious disease after another, growing weaker with each one. Sooner or later, they die. Though new drugs have extended the lives of those infected, AIDS cannot be cured, and there is no vaccine.

The disease came to medical attention between October 1980 and May 1981. The first victims were young homosexual men who had been healthy until they became infected.[3] In the United States, the disease seemed to attack only gay men at first. The first known case of heterosexual transmission in this country appeared in 1983. The victim was a woman whose husband

**When public health and safety are at stake, the guiding principle is the greatest good for the greatest number.**

had been sexually active in Africa. There, AIDS had already emerged and was running rampant among people of both sexes and all ages.

In 1984, scientists in the United States and France isolated HIV, the virus that causes AIDS. This led to a test that could detect HIV antibodies in blood and blood products. The FDA rushed it through the approval process and cleared it in 1985. Infection from contaminated blood products began to decline in the United States.

HIV/AIDS continued to strike injectable drug users who shared needles and people who had unprotected sex with infected partners. Unlike typhoid, AIDS cannot be spread by casual contact. In spite of this, AIDS victims often found themselves the targets of public hatred.

In one case, three brothers with hemophilia, a condition in which the blood does not clot normally, became HIV-positive through blood transfusions. The boys were not allowed to enter public school; the whole family endured repeated threats. Finally, an arsonist torched their home, forcing them to leave the area.

People with HIV/AIDS were evicted from their apartments, fired from their jobs, cast aside by their friends and families.

They ran up huge medical bills and had to cope with the knowledge that they were dying.

Their plight became a legal, ethical, and civil rights issue. Courts in several states applied existing antidiscrimination laws to people with HIV. The cases included hospitals and mortuaries that denied services to HIV-positive people, schools that excluded HIV-positive children, and companies that fired HIV-positive workers.

In the late 1980s, the government banned discrimination against federal workers with HIV. The FDA streamlined its testing procedures to get new drugs out to the people who needed them. It also allowed AIDS patients to import nonapproved drugs for their own use.[4] Following the FDA lead, AIDS researchers put their experiments on a fast track. Public health agencies offered free testing for anyone who wanted it, no questions asked.

That was not enough for some people. In 1987, vice president George H. W. Bush and others called for nationwide mandatory testing. Gay groups and human rights organizations argued that such a program would be useless. It would not save lives; there was no cure for HIV. Testing would make people with HIV into pariahs, or social outcasts.

Those who favored testing argued that people who knew they had HIV might change behaviors such as sharing drug needles and having unprotected sex. This argument did not result in mandatory HIV/AIDS testing.

## AIDS, Morality, and Public Health

Instead of widespread testing, public health agencies began promoting simple precautions to slow the spread of HIV. In hospitals and medical clinics, doctors and nurses wore latex gloves to examine patients. They put used syringes into special biohazard containers, so that no one would be stuck by a contaminated needle. In college and professional sports, players with bleeding injuries had to leave the game until the bleeding could be controlled. The public readily accepted these measures as both sensible and necessary.

This was not the case when AIDS prevention clashed with conservative ideas of morality. For example, Surgeon General C. Everett Koop promoted condom use to prevent transmission of HIV during sexual activity. Public health agencies set up needle exchange programs. Anyone could exchange a dirty needle for a clean one, without fear of arrest.

Howls of protest greeted these programs. Religious and social conservatives insisted that illicit sex and illegal drugs were moral issues. Society should seek to eliminate them altogether, not make them safer.

**The AIDS quilt, made in honor of those who have died of the disease, on display in Washington, D.C. In the 1980s, controversy arose over the question of mandatory HIV/AIDS testing.**

People involved in AIDS prevention and treatment did not agree. Their job was to prevent a deadly disease, not to stand in judgment of its victims. The job grew more urgent with every passing day. By 2004, more than a million Americans were living with HIV.[5] Worldwide, the number infected had jumped from 10 million in 1990 to more than 39 million in 2004.[6]

## The Hidden Dangers of Genetic Engineering

The AIDS epidemic produced a new argument against genetic engineering. The reasoning was simple: AIDS came out of nowhere and started killing people. What if somebody accidentally created a pathogen even worse than HIV?

In 2001, a group of Australian researchers unwittingly demonstrated that such a thing might actually happen. They had been looking for a way to make mice infertile (incapable of producing offspring). Instead, they created a virus that killed every mouse in the laboratory by destroying its immune system.

These researchers were not behaving unethically; risk is a necessary part of the scientific process. An act becomes unethical when it crosses the line between risk and recklessness.

Scientists sometimes disagree about where to place that line, but most do agree that risk should be proportional to possible benefit. Finding a cure for cancer or AIDS, for example, would be worth more risk than developing a new remedy for the common cold.

One project that became controversial was the search for the pathogen that caused the great influenza pandemic of 1918. Dr. Michael Katze, a microbiologist at the University of Washington, called this strain of influenza "the most deadly infectious disease in the history of mankind," noting that it killed at least forty million people worldwide.[7]

The virus did its killing and then disappeared; no one knew what had made it so deadly. Then in 1997, scientists from the Armed Forces Institute of Pathology began studying preserved tissue samples of 1918 victims. By comparing the 1918 strain to other influenza genes, they confirmed that it was different—like nothing seen before or since.

By the autumn of 2003, scientists had gone beyond studying the genetic makeup of the virus. They were reconstructing it, bringing it back to life. Their stated goal was to test present-day antiviral drugs against the 1918 strain. They wanted to be sure they could kill it, should the need ever arise.

Others argued against reconstruction on the grounds that the risks of the project far outweigh the potential benefits. Edward Hammond of the Sunshine Project, a biotechnology watchdog group in Austin, Texas, pointed out scientific and ethical problems with reconstruction: "This project could create a new bug that infects someone in the lab who then walks out at the end of the day and, literally, kills tens of millions of people."[8]

## Ethics, Agriculture, and Biotechnology

Accidentally releasing a doomsday virus is just one disquieting possibility of the genomic age. Some people fear that tainting the food supply could be another. They are dismayed at the very thought of genetically engineered (GE) foods, or genetically modified organisms (GMOs), as they are also called. Supporters of genetic engineering argue that it can adapt plants to grow in inhospitable environments, increase crop yield, and eventually put an end to world hunger.

Genetic engineering changes a plant's genetic code through a process called recombinant DNA, or gene splicing. This technique can make plants more adaptable to various climates or soils and more resistant to common pests. It can make the food supply more nutritious by adding vitamins and minerals. It can even create plants that will produce vaccines or medicines.

In their quest for maximum benefits from genetically engineered crops, developers have created some odd combinations. For example, to make tomatoes more resistant to cold weather, scientists added a gene from a fish that lives in icy, arctic waters. They have also put chicken genes into potatoes, human genes into rice, and rat genes into soybeans.

This may sound odd or dangerous, but developers contend that gene-swapping is safe. They point out that living organisms naturally share many genes. Careful testing can ensure the safety of transgenic, or genetically altered, crops.

In spite of these reassurances, many people remain unconvinced. They worry about contaminating the food supply with new and possibly dangerous crops. Some simply feel uneasy at the thought of putting fish genes into tomatoes.

In England, and later in the United States, opponents dubbed GE crops "Frankenfoods," after the fictional doctor who created a monster in his secret laboratory. With tongue firmly in cheek, British journalist Tony Levene wondered if these Frankenstein foods would "cause two-headed rabbits to sprout in fields otherwise denuded of life except for giant tomatoes?"[9]

One point of contention concerning GE foods is that seeds and pollen can spread, contaminating crops in non-GE fields. In Canada, GE contamination of natural crops triggered an unexpected controversy.

The Monsanto Company, a major developer of bioengineered seed, held patents on its GE varieties. This protected the company's rights to the process. No one could make, sell, or use the seed without payment to Monsanto. Anyone who did so was guilty of patent infringement.

The trouble began when "Roundup Ready" seeds drifted into non-GE fields. "Roundup" was the brand name for Monsanto's powerful herbicide, or weed killer. With plants that could withstand Roundup, farmers could spray their fields, knowing they would kill weeds, not crops.

Farmers who grew natural crops found themselves in an odd predicament. If Roundup Ready seed drifted into their fields, Monsanto could charge them with patent infringement.

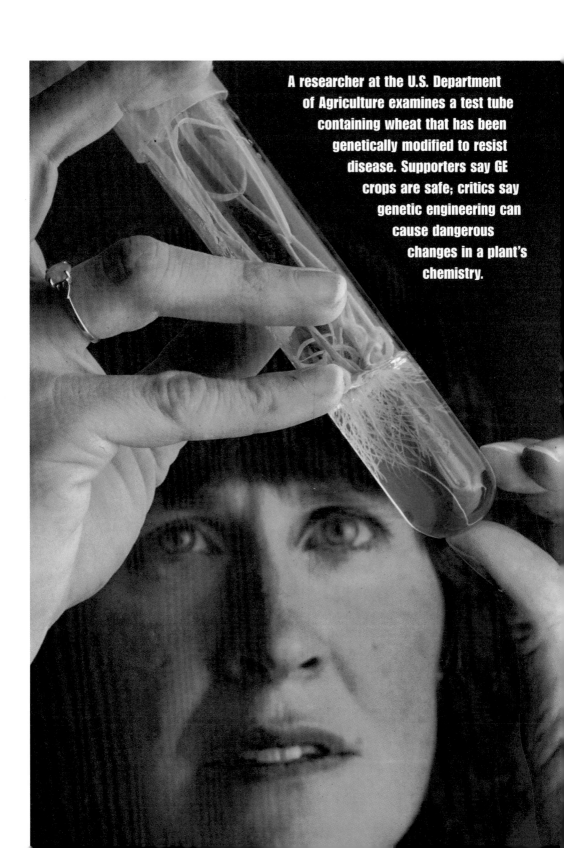

A researcher at the U.S. Department of Agriculture examines a test tube containing wheat that has been genetically modified to resist disease. Supporters say GE crops are safe; critics say genetic engineering can cause dangerous changes in a plant's chemistry.

The company did just that when Canadian farmer Percy Schmeiser found Roundup Ready plants in his canola fields. Monsanto had created a careful licensing structure. It charged a "technology fee" of $15 per acre. In addition, licensees agreed to use Monsanto's Roundup weed killer rather than less expensive competitors, and also agree to buy fresh seed every year. This meant that they could not save seed from one season to another, something farmers have been doing since humankind first began to till the soil.

Schmeiser had never agreed to Monsanto's terms, nor did he want their Roundup Ready canola in his fields. He refused to pay the company's fine, arguing that no company should have rights to any seed spread through the environment:

> This gene doesn't make the plant grow. It doesn't make it green, or produce seed. All it does is keep the plant from dying if you spray Roundup on it. And yet they're saying that even though nature and other people created canola, because they put one gene in it, everything is theirs.[10]

The dispute between Schmeiser and Monsanto ended up in court. For six long years, it went through suits, countersuits, and appeals. On May 21, 2004, the Canadian Supreme Court affirmed Monsanto's patent rights. At the same time, it gave Schmeiser a personal victory: he did not have to pay Monsanto anything because "he did not profit from the presence of Roundup Ready canola in his fields."[11]

For farmers' rights organizations, that mostly symbolic victory was not enough. They vowed to keep the issue alive. To them, the case was not about one independent farmer battling a giant corporation. According to Terry Boehm of the National Farmers Union, it "was about preserving age-old agricultural practices such as seed saving and protecting farmers from being held responsible for the . . . contamination of our farm fields."[12]

To Monsanto, the case was about protecting patents. By the standards of corporate culture, this was both ethical and necessary.

GE food supporters argue that transgenic plants may someday feed the hungry millions of the world. Engineered seed can not only increase crop yields, but allow farmers to grow food in poor soil and inhospitable climates.

Few GE opponents would argue against feeding the hungry, but they want to be sure it is done safely. They fear that human tinkering with the code of life may one day destroy the very thing it is trying to save.

The experts are as divided as the rest of society. Geneticist and organic physicist Mae-Wan Ho cautions that "Genetic engineering is *inherently* dangerous, because it greatly expands the scope for horizontal gene transfer and recombination, precisely the processes that create new viruses and bacteria that cause disease epidemics, and trigger cancer in cells."[13] [Italics in original]

Nobel prizewinner Dr. Norman Borlaug argues the opposite side, stating that the only way to feed the growing world population is for farmers to "have access to current high-yielding crop production methods as well as new biotechnological breakthroughs that can increase the yields, dependability and nutritional quality of our basic food crops."[14]

With these fundamental scientific and ethical issues, the twenty-first century is likely to see more conflict between those who press for rapid technological progress and those who say that biotech is moving too far, too fast.

# 4    Ethics at the Beginning of Life

Having children is not just a biological process. It is surrounded by a host of laws, rules, religious customs, and moral concerns. Over the years, these standards have adapted to social change and shifting moral values.

In the mid-twentieth century in most societies, birth control, abortion, and pregnancy outside of marriage were the most controversial reproductive issues. An unmarried woman who got pregnant was considered by many to have committed a sin; if she had an abortion, she committed a crime. If she kept her child, it would be a constant, living reminder of her disgrace. If she gave the child up for adoption, she might feel the loss her whole life.

Today, much of that has changed. The sexual behavior of consenting adults is becoming a matter of conscience rather than a point of law. Some people consider this a healthy development. Others consider it a moral disaster. The two sides do agree on one thing: a single, small pill helped to trigger the changes.

## The Battle for Birth Control

The first birth control pill won FDA approval in 1960 and promptly created a public debate. The idea of taking a pill to allow sexual activity without the risk of pregnancy offended many people. Several states already banned contraceptives such as the diaphragm and the condom. They simply added the pill to that list.

In 1961, Estelle Griswold opened a birth control clinic in New Haven, Connecticut. She expected to be arrested, and the local authorities did not disappoint her. The case went all the way to the United States Supreme Court, which ruled that bans on birth control violated the right to marital privacy.

That ruling made the pill more or less respectable, but only for married women. Unmarried women did not win the right to use the contraceptives until 1972, when the case of *Eisenstadt* v. *Baird* extended the right of privacy to them.

Not everyone took the Supreme Court decision as the final word. Though unmarried women had a legal right to use the pill, social and religious conservatives still considered it immoral. In their view, doctors who prescribed the pill were unethical; women who used it were sinful.

Social liberals argued that legalized birth control did not destroy traditional values; it simply took the government out of the business of enforcing them.[1]

## The Abortion Debate

On January 22, 1973, the Supreme Court issued another landmark decision. In the case of *Roe* v. *Wade*, the court held that a woman has a constitutional right to have an abortion during the first three months of pregnancy.

The decision caused a nationwide furor. Women's rights activists celebrated a milestone victory. Abortion opponents mourned, because in their view the Court had just legalized a form of murder.

Abortion has always been a polarizing issue; many people take sides that allow little or no room for compromise. They do agree on one thing: the abortion debate hinges on when and how a fetus becomes a person. Those who think personhood begins at birth are more likely to support abortion than those who think it begins at the moment of conception.

Some hardline opponents of abortion consider themselves ethically justified in using violence to further their cause. They have harrassed women seeking abortion, bombed clinics, and assassinated doctors who work in them.

For example, domestic terrorist Eric Rudolph, who is best known for bombing the 1996 Olympic games in Atlanta, Georgia, left a trail of abortion clinic bombings in his wake. In the summer of 2005, Rudolph was sentenced to four life terms without parole, guaranteeing that he would die in prison.

**People on both sides of the abortion issue agree on one thing: The debate hinges on when and how a fetus becomes a person.**

Many antiabortionists are outspoken in their opposition to this kind of violence. To them, killing adults to protest the killing of fetuses is not only immoral and unethical, it does not make sense. Right-to-life advocate James M. Wallace constructed an argument against violence in a letter to the Greensboro, North Carolina *News & Record*:

> Though I am . . . opposed to . . . abortion . . . I am always deeply disturbed by acts of violence against [clinics] and abortionists. I am especially troubled when these acts result in death or injury. My . . . hope is that every criminal responsible for such acts is caught, prosecuted, convicted, and punished to the fullest extent of

the law. Terrorism, murder, and arson are horrific crimes and are not appropriate expressions of political protest.[2]

## Assisted Reproduction

While the battle over abortion raged, another issue was waiting in the wings: assisted reproduction. The controversy began with John and Lesley Brown of Oldham, England.

The Browns had spent nine years trying to have a baby, with no success. Then they consulted Dr. Patrick Steptoe, who was experimenting with in vitro fertilization (IVF). (*In vitro* means "in glass.") The glass in question was not the famous test tube of modern legend. It was a small, round petri dish.

Steptoe and physiologist Robert Edwards began by extracting one of Lesley Brown's eggs. They fertilized it with her husband's sperm and put the embryo into a nutrient solution. When the embryo was ready, they placed it into Lesley Brown's uterus.

On July 25, 1978, Lesley Brown gave birth to a healthy baby girl, who was later named Louise. The birth caused a sensation in the tabloid press and raised many issues in the scientific community. Some scientists called the achievement "trivial" and "a cookbook thing." Others wrote it off as a "cheap stunt," or predicted that unnamed "dangerous events" would follow the birth.[3]

The birth of Louise Brown raised a new set of ethical questions. Most revolved around the fact that IVF had replaced a natural process with an artificial one. This put human beings in control of a process that many believed rightly belonged to God or to nature. Some feared that this meddling with nature would produce damaged or deformed children.

Conservative theologian Paul Ramsey and others claimed that embryos were "persons" and IVF an experimental procedure. Therefore, subjecting embryos to IVF violated their right to informed consent.

**This fertilized egg has divided so that it forms a two-cell embryo. Controversy over ethics at the beginning of life often hinges on whether people believe personhood begins at conception or at birth.**

Except for the manner of her conception, Louise was a normal child. She inherited her genetic structure from her parents in the ordinary way. She grew up, got married, and had children of her own. By her twenty-fifth birthday in 2003, in vitro fertilization had produced more than a million babies conceived in clinics throughout the world.[4]

## The Ethics of Assisted Reproduction

Despite these accomplishments, IVF technology does have its drawbacks: it is complex, expensive, and not always effective. According to figures from the Centers for Disease Control and

Prevention (CDC) for the year 2000, 30.7 percent of IVF attempts resulted in pregnancy, and 85 percent of those pregnancies produced live births. Average cost per attempt was $12,500, and some couples made multiple attempts.[5] Some of those couples eventually had babies; some did not.

Because of the expense and the difficulty, IVF is rarely the first choice for couples who want to have a baby. Intrauterine insemination (IU) is easier and a great deal cheaper, at about $1,000 per attempt. In this process, sperm is inserted directly into the uterus. After that, biotechnology gives way to nature. Conception and pregnancy occur normally if they occur at all.

Assisted reproduction is changing the meaning of parenthood. Surrogate, or substitute, mothers bear children for other people. Fertility clinics harvest and sell human eggs, establish sperm banks, create embryos, and freeze them for later use.

## The Fate of Stored Embryos

What happens to those leftover embryos in cold storage tanks? That question has touched off many an ethical argument. The embryos could be donated for adoption, used for research, destroyed, or simply held in storage for an indefinite period.

The extreme positions on each side of this issue mirror those on abortion. People who believe that life begins at conception claim that destroying an embryo is murder. Those who believe that life begins at birth generally see no problem with disposing of unwanted embryos.

The fate of frozen embryos belonging to Mario and Elsa Rios made headlines when the couple died in a 1983 plane crash. The Australian fertility clinic that created the embryos sought legal help in deciding their fate. After lengthy debate about the ethical issues involved, the Australian parliament ordered the embryos preserved until they could be adopted.

This decision did not solve the problem, but neither did it offend anyone's moral scruples. The case disappeared from the headlines, the embryos remained in cold storage, and the ethical conflict remained unchanged. No one came forward to adopt the embryos.

At the time of the Rios case, embryo adoption was almost unknown. By the early twenty-first century, it had become more common. There are even agencies that will handle embryo adoption, placing embryos with prospective parents. As in ordinary adoption, the children have no genetic relationship to their adoptive parents.

Many who choose embryo adoption have not been able to conceive, even with the help of modern science. Some may carry a genetic defect that they do not want to pass on to their offspring. Others may simply be too old for natural parenthood.

## Ethics and Older Mothers

On January 17, 2005, sixty-six-year-old Adriana Iliescu of Bucharest, Romania, gave birth to a baby girl. The media immediately dubbed Iliescu "the world's oldest mom." This is true in a limited way. Iliescu's eggs were not fertile because of her age. Her doctor used donor sperm and donor eggs to create the embryos he implanted.

Iliescu's motherhood drew more criticism than praise. The Romanian Orthodox Church called it "selfish." The *National* newspaper noted that Iliescu will be eighty when her daughter becomes a teenager. The Romanian Health Ministry submitted a bill to parliament, forbidding "medically assisted human reproduction . . . in cases of infertility caused by age."[6]

## Surrogates: Having Someone Else's Child

The use of surrogate mothers is perhaps even more controversial than impregnating senior citizens. Generally, would-be parents use a surrogate if the wife is sterile or unable to carry a child to term. In the first case, the surrogate's egg and the husband's sperm may be used. The wife will not be genetically related to the baby. In the second case, the wife's egg and husband's sperm are used. Thus, the baby will be the biological offspring of both parents, and the surrogate will not be genetically related to the baby.

These tangled relationships can create legal, ethical, and personal issues. Generally, the prospective parents make a contract with the surrogate, agreeing to pay her a certain amount of money. The surrogate agrees to hand over the child to them and waive all parental rights.

These contracts must be carefully worded so that none of the parties involved are buying or selling a baby. To do this, the prospective parents pay the surrogate's medical expenses and

**Frozen sperm is stored in a tank filled with liquid nitrogen; it is removed, thawed, and used in IVF. Because of the expense and the high failure rate, IVF is not usually the first treatment choice for infertile couples.**

sometimes her living expenses as well. In addition to this, they agree to pay for her time.

In the early 1980s, surrogacy was so new that nobody knew exactly how to handle it. The unanswered questions led to a headline-grabbing dispute that became known as the case of Baby M.

The situation began on February 5, 1985, when Mary Beth Whitehead agreed to be a surrogate mother for William and Elizabeth Stern. Under the terms of the agreement, Whitehead would be artificially inseminated with the sperm of William Stern and give birth to his baby. The Sterns agreed to pay her ten thousand dollars for her services. In return, Whitehead agreed to turn the baby over to the Sterns and give up her parental rights.

By the time Baby M was born on March 27, 1986, Mary Beth Whitehead had changed her mind. Instead of giving up the baby, she claimed her parental rights.

In doing this, she violated her contract with the Sterns. They sued, launching a case that involved two competing views of the situation. On the one hand, it was a child custody issue; on the other, it was a contract dispute. These require different ethical approaches.

Child custody is intensely personal; it raises questions about relationships, feelings, and moral values. Contract disputes deal with facts and figures and are often about money. Did person A break his or her agreement? If so, what are the damages to person B? Court proceedings focus on establishing blame.

Ethical conflicts about parenthood do not fit well into this mold. The case dragged through the courts for more than a year, finally ending in February 1988. The ruling gave custody of Baby M to William Stern.

Later, Mary Beth Whitehead went back to court to get visiting rights. In the spring of 1989, the court granted her "unsupervised, uninterrupted, liberal visitation."[7]

To avoid future conflict, the court included what amounted to a visitation schedule. It established everything from a schedule of weekends through the year to holidays and summer vacations.

Many who supported surrogacy argued that the Baby M case distorted the true picture. Before Baby M, some eight hundred to one thousand surrogate mothers had given birth to somebody else's baby. All but four of those cases went through without incident.[8]

## "What Is a Mother?"

According to Gregory Pence, assisted reproduction in general and the Baby M case in particular raised "a basic philosophical question." That question was "What is a mother?"

> In . . . surrogacy, who is the real mother: the egg donor, the gesta-tor who carries the fetus to term, or the woman who raises the child? Perhaps the best answer is simply, "Improper question." In other words, perhaps we need not conclude that one woman must be the "real" mother.[9]

Those who favor a businesslike approach to surrogacy might disagree with the idea that the "gestator" is the legal mother of the child she carries. Her job is *not* to think of herself as the mother. Her job is to give birth, hand the baby over to its parents, collect her fee, and go on her way. Some people are horrified by this attitude. By their standards, it reduces childbearing to a demeaning rent-a-womb transaction.

Professor of religion and social ethics Thomas A. Shannon goes further. He contends that surrogacy contracts amount to baby-selling: "The fulfillment of the surrogate contract . . . is 'the production of an acceptable child who is then taken by the biological father.' When this occurs, a fee is exchanged. This is exchanging cash for a baby."[10] Buying and selling babies is not only unethical, it is illegal.

Shannon offers an illustration from attorney Angela Holder:

When you go into a store, ask for an item, and pay for it, when the clerk hands it to you, you have bought it and it is yours. You have not purchased the services of the clerk, though to be sure some of the payment is the basis of his or her salary. You have purchased the item. . . . If someone would try to take it away from you, this would be an act of theft for which that individual could be arrested and prosecuted. In surrogacy, cash changes hands and the baby changes families.[11]

Supporters of surrogacy argue that nobody is buying or selling babies; the parents are paying the surrogate for her services. Giving the baby to its new parents completes the contract, so the surrogate is entitled to payment.

Though paid surrogacy remains controversial, many people put surrogacy that is freely given into a different ethical category. In "altruistic surrogacy," as it is called, the surrogate receives no payment. This typically occurs within families, when one relative wants to help another have children. In one such case, fifty-five-year-old Tina Cade of Richmond, Virginia, gave birth to her own grandchildren. In December 2004, she delivered triplets, the genetic offspring of her daughter and son-in-law, Camille and Jason Hammond.

## Wrongful Birth/Wrongful Life

The biotechnology that lets grandmothers give birth to triplets may be wondrous, but it is not infallible. Genetic testing can detect a number of defects in the first trimester (three months) of fetal development. This gives the parents a choice: they can continue the pregnancy to term, or they can abort the fetus and try again.

To make this hard choice, parents rely upon the doctor's judgment. If that judgment is wrong, the impact on their lives can be devastating.

Mistakes in prenatal testing have triggered lawsuits charging wrongful birth or wrongful life. In a wrongful birth suit,

Assisted reproduction has developed enormously since the first in vitro fertilization in 1978. High-tech methods have enabled many people to become parents who otherwise would not have had a baby.

the parents claim that a doctor or other medical professional misinformed them; had they known the truth, they would have terminated the pregnancy.

Wrongful life suits are brought by the child or someone acting on his or her behalf. The suit alleges that life itself is the wrong inflicted on the client. This amounts to saying that the child should never have existed.

To outsiders, this might seem harsh and unfeeling. To some parents of severely disabled children, it can seem entirely reasonable. For example, Richard and Helen Schirmer knew that Helen carried a dormant genetic disorder called trisomy 22. It causes severe mental retardation and crippling physical disabilities.

When Helen Schirmer got pregnant, she went through genetic testing, planning to abort the fetus if it tested positive for trisomy 22. The doctors assured the Schirmers that the fetus did not have the defective gene; their baby would be born healthy. On the strength of that information, the Schirmers continued the pregnancy.

The Schirmers were devastated when Helen gave birth to a son with trisomy 22. Matthew Schirmer was severely retarded and physically disabled. At the age of six, he still could not stand, walk, or even crawl. He never learned how to talk, how to dress himself, feed himself, or take a bath.

The Schirmers sued, blaming medical negligence for the inaccurate test results. The complaint went nowhere, mostly because it did not fit the standard definition of malpractice. Helen's doctor had not caused Matthew's disabilities, nor had he made them worse. Legally, he was not at fault for those disabilities. The only injury to the Schirmer family was that Matthew had been born. Current law does not allow such a position.

## New Technology Yields Ethical Challenges

In spite of ethical issues, moral outrage, and just plain fear, biotechnology is reshaping the way human beings deal with reproductive issues. Some predict that this will mechanize and dehumanize this most basic of human functions.

Others argue that these problems and challenges do not discredit the entire field of reproductive technology. It has many benefits to offer humankind.

Though an error in the Schirmer case led to tragedy, genetic testing has helped thousands avoid passing on genetic defects to the next generation. Because of biotechnology, scientists can ensure that healthy eggs are implanted during IVF. They can detect and repair certain birth defects while the baby is still in the womb, thus avoiding an emotionally charged decision about whether or not to have an abortion.

There have always been ethical challenges in medicine, and there have always been risks. As Dr. Peter Rheinstein of the U.S. Food and Drug Administration points out, "Any medicine that's strong enough to help you also has the power to hurt you if you don't take it right."[12]

The same might be said for the latest biotechnology; it can be risky. It can also challenge existing moral standards. However, if informed people are allowed to make free choices about reproductive issues, society can benefit from biotechnology and still keep it on a human scale.

**5**

# Distributing Medical Resources

The distribution of medical care raises a host of practical, economic, and ethical issues. Much of the latest technology is in short supply; most of it is expensive. This means that not everyone who needs treatment will receive it. Somebody must decide who gets what and in what order.

## Triage and Treatment

High-tech advances in diagnosis and treatment have not replaced all older methods. Emergency medicine relies on the time-honored technique of *triage*, which means "to sort." French army medics developed it in the early 1800s to classify battlefield casualties so that the most seriously injured who had some chance of recovery would receive immediate attention. Triage was so successful that it became standard practice for rescue workers in disaster areas and medical personnel in hospital emergency rooms.

In disaster areas, triage teams often use color-coded tags to indicate each patient's condition: red means critical; yellow, urgent; and green, nonurgent. Finally, a black tag indicates that treatment would be futile, or useless. Emergency workers take special care before acknowledging futility. Black-tagged victims will be left to die without receiving further attention.

In emergency rooms, nurses usually perform triage, checking incoming patients and assigning priorities. The sickest people go directly to treatment rooms; those with less serious complaints are sent to the waiting room. On a busy night, lower priority patients may wait many hours to see a doctor.

Dr. Robert Derlet, Chief of Emergency Medicine at the University of California (Davis) Medical Center, describes emergency room triage as a "high-risk activity."[1] The need to evaluate many people in the shortest possible time in a crowded emergency room can lead to mistakes. The triage nurse may misinterpret a symptom or fail to notice some detail that will prove to be important. Dr. Derlet recommends periodic reevaluation of patients assigned to the waiting room to determine any changes in condition.

This precaution can help catch mistakes before they do harm. However, it cannot eliminate them altogether. Almost every emergency room has its share of disasters, or near-disasters. In one case, a forty-three-year-old woman came into the emergency room complaining of a headache. Though she had a temperature of 101.2° F, her blood pressure, pulse, and respiration tested normal.

The triage nurse sent the patient to the waiting room. Four hours later, the woman had a seizure. Her temperature soared to 104.5° F. She was admitted to the hospital with spinal meningitis, a serious and often deadly infection of the membranes enclosing the brain and spinal cord.

Honest mistakes, even serious ones, are not ethical issues. Ethics can help to determine right and wrong; it can provide standards for making sound decisions. It cannot make human beings perfect, or error-proof every decision.

## Distributing Resources for Beginnings and Endings

Triage requires quick judgment calls under emergency conditions. Caring for premature babies and the frail elderly calls for different decision-making skills. To decide on a course of treatment, doctors have to consider available resources, benefits, risks, and prognosis, or probable outcome, for the patient.

The very young and the very old use the most resources. For example, in the first year of life a premature baby costs insurers $41,610, nearly fifteen times more than the $2,830 needed for a full-term baby.[2] Because of disabilities associated with prematurity, children who were premature are more likely to require continuing treatment, so even after the first year, they are usually more costly to raise than children who were born full term.

Medicare, the government health care program for the elderly, spends $99 billion every year to provide care during the last year of life. That is one third of the program's total budget of nearly $300 billion.[3]

Philosopher Daniel Callahan favors limiting health care for the elderly. This should be "fair, humane, and sensitive to . . . their special requirements and dignity. . . . Government has a duty, based on our collective social obligations, to help people live out a natural life span but not to help medically extend life beyond that point."[4]

Some people find Callahan's view insensitive, if not unethical. Others call it realistic. Modern western cultures have treated death as the enemy, to be fought and conquered at any cost.

Callahan traced this idea back to the late 1800s, "when medicine started becoming effective in saving life."[5]

Through the twentieth century, the battle against death intensified: here a new procedure, a new medicine; there a research project aimed at curing or at least controlling the diseases and the frailties of aging. With this mindset, old age becomes a painful reminder that sooner or later, that enemy will win.

In some cultures, old age is a time for coming to terms with life and preparing for death. The elderly get ready to face the greatest mystery of human existence, and that task brings purpose to their lives. When the task is complete, prolonging life for additional days, weeks, or months rarely becomes an issue.

For example, the Hindu tradition teaches that medicine can only go so far in healing. It is not unethical to acknowledge this, or to accept the fact that death will "win."

An article in *Hinduism Today* stated: "Prolonging the life of the individual body" when the person is beyond striving and ready to die "is to incarcerate, to jail, to place that person in prison. Ayurvedic [traditional Indian] medicine seeks to keep a person healthy and strong, but not to interfere with the process of death."[6]

## Evaluating Patients for Organ Transplants

Whatever the age of the patients involved, allocating, or distributing, scarce resources is one of the most difficult jobs in medicine. This is especially true when the resources in question are human organs. Candidates for transplant undergo a careful examination by evaluators who examine their entire medical history. The evaluators consider factors such as age, probable life span, other medical conditions, and destructive habits like alcohol abuse, drug use, and smoking. They use objective criteria to ensure that all applicants are judged by the same standards.

For example, in considering life span, a forty-year-old with no other health problems will probably outlive a seventy-year-old with diabetes. That is not a value judgment; it is factual statement that can be verified by statistics.

Some people might be inclined to reject applicants whose past behavior has contributed to their illness. The rules and standards of the organ donation program forbid this. A recovering alcoholic who needs a new liver or an ex-smoker who needs a new lung have the same rights as other candidates.

Close-up of a heart transplant performed on a child. A number of factors, such as age and medical history, are used in evaluating who should receive the scarce organs available for transplantation.

Evaluators might refuse an alcoholic who continues to drink, or a smoker who continues to smoke, on grounds that their habits shorten their life expectancy. What evaluators cannot do is make moral judgments about who is, and who is not, worthy of a second chance at life.

According to Dr. John Fung of the Thomas E. Starzl Transplantation Institute, the dangers of moral judgments go beyond the fate of any one applicant:

> The concept of "who should get an organ" should be based primarily on medical issues. When one [considers] values . . . such as social worth, social status, financial means, intelligence, etc., the decision . . . becomes subjective, and not objective. It is impossible to quantify [measure or count] these values. . . . For example, should the president of a corporation receive a transplant over a blue-collar worker? Should a university professor receive a transplant over someone who has only a grade school education? These decisions introduce . . . personal values into the decision-making process.[7]

Applicants who are approved go onto a waiting list with thousands of other candidates. When an organ becomes available, first consideration goes to patients who are the closest match, followed by those who have been waiting the longest and those who are critically ill.[8]

To match donor and recipient, blood types must be compatible. A cross-match test must be negative, meaning that the patient's antibodies will not kill donor cells. Even with a perfect match, transplants take a toll on the recipient's body.

The immune system treats the new organ as a foreign substance. Left alone, it will reject and eventually destroy the "invader." To prevent this, recipients must take antirejection drugs for the rest of their lives at a cost of around $15,000 a year.

## Shortages and Controversies

Making the waiting list is only the first hurdle for someone needing a transplant. It is a long way from actually obtaining an organ. Despite programs that encourage people to donate, the shortage of organs is a nationwide problem.

According to the United Network for Organ Sharing (UNOS), 87,915 Americans were on the waiting list in January 2005. In that same month, doctors completed 4,367 transplants, while national transplant networks received a total of 2,263 donor organs. Each day, an average of seventeen people died, still waiting for a transplant.[9]

Every now and then, some new controversy will focus public attention on the shortage. For example, in May 2003, a doctor at the Oregon state prison suggested that death row inmate Horacio Reyes-Camarena was a good candidate for a kidney transplant. The doctor's remarks stirred public outrage. Reyes-Camarena was condemned to die for a particularly vicious knife attack that left one woman dead and another gravely injured.

Reyes-Camarena was already receiving dialysis, a procedure that filters impurities from the blood when the kidneys can no longer function. Some argued that a transplant made medical and financial sense. It would restore kidney function and make dialysis unnecessary. It would also save money over Reyes-Camarena's expected life span on death row.

With automatic appeals, he would not face execution for at least ten years. Over that period, his dialysis treatments would cost more than a million dollars. A transplant would cost about $350,000, including the surgery itself and $15,000 a year for antirejection drugs.

The numbers may have favored a transplant, but the people of Oregon did not. Opponents argued that giving a priceless organ to a death-row inmate was simply wrong—and no laws or rules or ethical codes could make it right.

Still, inmates have rights: "We really do have to provide for ... [prisoners'] care," said district attorney Joshua Marquis. "So it's more of a moral issue than a legal one. ... Personally, I find it abhorrent that someone like Mr. Reyes-Camarena could receive a transplant before anybody who is more deserving."[10]

Steven Shelton, medical director at the Oregon Department of Corrections, decided to put the issue to rest. In June 2003, he convened a panel of doctors to consider Reyes-Camarena's transplant.

They denied the request, saying that Reyes-Camarena did not meet standards established by the state. The case disappeared from the headlines and the six o'clock news, and the heated debate over transplant ethics once more faded into the background.

## Bioethics and the Bottom Line

Of all the ways to determine who receives what care, ability to pay is perhaps the harshest. The American health care system is one of the costliest in the world. According to a report from the Boston University School of Public Health, spending on health care in the United States is projected to reach $1.9 trillion in 2005.[11]

The impact on individuals can be devastating. If not for health insurance and government-funded programs like Medicare and Medicaid, only the wealthy few could afford even the most basic care.

According to Sheila McLean, a professor of Law and Ethics in Medicine at Glasgow University:

> In contemporary society, the inability to obtain insurance for life and health purposes can mean the difference between a life with quality and a life with little or none. . . . it may mean . . . that increasing numbers of people fall outside of any safety net; that the elderly will not be treated; that [prenatal] care will not be undertaken; that people will die for the lack of basic care.[12]

The high cost of medical care begins long before patients come into the picture. It starts with companies that spend millions of dollars developing new drugs or state-of-the-art testing equipment. Doctors charge for prescribing the drugs and ordering the tests. Pharmacies charge for dispensing the drugs, and hospitals charge for conducting the tests.

**Doctors, nurses, and EMTs rush an accident victim into treatment. The American health care system is among the costliest in the world; if not for insurance and government funding, only the wealthy could afford care.**

By the time these advances reach patients, they carry a high price tag. This not only creates economic issues, but legal and ethical ones as well. For example, cancer research costs millions of dollars each year; cancer diagnosis and treatment, millions more.

On the plus side of the ledger, this expenditure has saved many lives. Since the early 1990s, the death rate for cancer has dropped 1.5 percent per year for men and 0.8 percent for women.[13] These statistics include common malignancies such as lung, breast, and colon cancer.

Early detection has become the watchword of cancer diagnosis. Screening tests detect cancer in its earliest stages. However, they can also give false positives that lead to expensive and sometimes dangerous diagnostic tests.

It would be a poor use of resources to screen every patient for every possible disease. Low-risk, fairly inexpensive tests can be wise precautions for high-risk patients: mammograms for women over fifty and lung X-rays for smokers.

Even the simplest tests may not be worthwhile for some patients. For example, testing a ninety-year-old man for prostate cancer would be useless. Even if the patient tested positive, he would not be a candidate for treatment. A man of that age would probably not live long enough for the cancer to produce symptoms. In any case, he would probably not survive the rigors of surgery, chemotherapy, or radiation. In this hypothetical case, the decision is straightforward: there are sound medical reasons for withholding treatment.

Increasingly, doctors have to plan treatment with one eye on medical necessity and the other on cost effectiveness. In many situations, health maintenance organizations (HMOs) and managed care programs require doctors to submit their treatment plans for approval. The insurance companies argue that cost control benefits everybody. Costs must be managed to keep the health care system from collapsing of its own weight. This means bottom-line thinking—balancing the patient's need for quality health care against the industry's need for profit. Even socialized, or government-funded, medicine must control costs.

Allocation of resources will be an inescapable part of twenty-first century medicine. Ethicists, health care professionals, attorneys, and others are creating ethical codes. Their goal is to ensure that decisions about medical care will be fair, even-handed, and based upon objective standards. Some fear that the system will overlook individuals. This may well be true, and unavoidable, due to the sheer size of the health care system. Local doctors, clinics, and even hospitals can continue relating to patients on a more personal level. Big Medicine will have to focus on the tried-and-true principle of the greatest good for the greatest number.

# 6     Ethics at the End of Life

Until the 1970s, a person was either alive or dead; it was not difficult to tell the difference. So long as the heart beat and the lungs moved air, the person was alive. When heartbeat and breathing stopped, a person was dead.

In the 1970s, artificial life support made it possible for people to exist in a kind of twilight world, somewhere between life and death. Machines keep the heart and lungs functioning; feeding tubes supply nutrients and fluids; catheters eliminate bodily waste.

Such patients are in a persistent vegetative state (PVS). They are awake but not aware. They can make sounds, but the sounds have no meaning. They can open their eyes and look around, but cannot interact with anything they see. They have no sense of their own identity.

## Persistent Vegetative States

In April 1975, twenty-one-year-old Karen Ann Quinlan lost consciousness and stopped breathing. She had been drinking alcohol at a party while also taking the tranquilizer Valium. Friends rushed her to a nearby hospital, where the staff placed her on a respirator and began tube feeding. By the time the hospital got her stabilized, lack of oxygen had damaged her brain beyond any chance of recovery.

At that time, most people had never heard of PVS. The term itself was new and the diagnostic criteria uncertain. Karen Quinlan became the prototype PVS patient: alive, awake, yet unaware of herself or her surroundings.

When Joseph and Julia Quinlan realized that their daughter was not going to recover, they asked the hospital to withdraw her respirator. That request launched a dispute that made headlines all over the nation.

Some called it murder. Others called it mercy, saying that Karen was not alive in any meaningful sense. Joseph Quinlan went to court, asking to be appointed Karen's guardian. This would give him the authority to have the respirator removed. The trial court denied his request. The Quinlans appealed to the New Jersey Supreme Court, which ruled that they could disconnect Karen's respirator.

The court ruling also allowed the Quinlans to disconnect Karen's feeding tube. This they could not bring themselves to do, nor did they think it necessary. They expected Karen to die soon after the respirator was removed. Instead, she began breathing on her own. Karen Quinlan lived another ten years, finally dying of pneumonia on June 11, 1985.

Her case raised a host of new ethical questions and created

widespread interest in end-of-life issues. People began creating advance health care directives.

## Advance Directives and Do-Not-Resuscitate Orders

An advance health care directive expresses the patient's wishes about medical care in extreme situations and when the patient cannot communicate. It deals with such things as artificial life support, catastrophic brain damage, and lingering terminal illness. No matter how thorough it may be, an advance directive cannot cover every possible circumstance. This leaves room for interpretation, and therefore for conflict.

For example, does a ban on artificial life support include routine use of a respirator during surgery? Does it mean that rescue teams cannot use simple CPR after an automobile accident? If the instructions are not clear, medical personnel must assume that the patient wants to live and treat him or her accordingly.

A do-not-resuscitate (DNR) order is simple and specific. It is a doctor's order directing medical personnel not to attempt CPR if the patient's heart or lungs should fail. Doctors consider a DNR order if they decide that the risk would be greater than the possible benefits. In a surprising number of cases, it is not.

Advanced CPR involves high-risk procedures such as electric shock, injection of stimulants directly into the heart, and even open heart massage.[1] Studies show that only 48 of every 100 patients who have advanced CPR will be successfully revived. Of those, only eleven will live long enough to get out of the hospital.[2] Their long-term survival rate averages just three years.[3]

These figures do not mean that doctors should never use advanced CPR, just that they should use it selectively. A generally healthy accident victim who has not been deprived of oxygen would be a good candidate for CPR. Frail and elderly patients would probably not survive the attempt, nor would dying patients on heavy doses of painkillers. Even if these

People can sign an advance health care directive to indicate the extent of the medical care they would like to receive. But even such directives cannot completely eliminate conflict.

patients did survive CPR, the extra hours, days, or weeks of life might be more a burden than a blessing.

## Medical Killing

The realization that extending life is not always a good thing produced the right-to-die movement. Some people claimed that a merciful death would be better than being kept alive indefinitely on artificial life support.

The word *euthanasia* literally means "good death." It is sometimes called "mercy killing," because it involves causing or allowing the death of a hopelessly ill individual in order to end his or her suffering.

Euthanasia can be voluntary or involuntary. When a mentally competent patient requests euthanasia, it is considered voluntary. When someone else makes the decision, the euthanasia is involuntary.

For many Americans, the very word "euthanasia" harkens back to Nazi Germany in the Second World War (1939–1945). Doctors killed those they considered "useless," starting with severely disabled newborns and young children. In a separate program, they killed adults with mental retardation, mental illness, or physical imperfections.

Few if any ethicists would call this euthanasia. Bob Lane, of the Institute of Practical Philosophy in Canada, maintained that "there is no relation at all between the Nazi 'euthanasia' program and modern debates about euthanasia. The Nazis, after all, used the word 'euthanasia' to camouflage mass murder."[4]

## Active and Passive Euthanasia

The terms "active" and "passive" refer to the role of the person who is caring for the patient. In active euthanasia, a doctor or other person directly causes the patient's death, perhaps by injecting a lethal drug. In passive euthanasia, caregivers allow the death to happen. This usually means withholding or discontinuing lifesaving treatments. For example, not resuscitating a patient could be considered a form of passive euthanasia. So could failure to treat a curable condition such as an infection that would respond to antibiotics. Some argue that removing a respirator, feeding tube, or other form of life support is as much an active procedure as giving the patient a lethal drug.

Many argue that the purpose of life support is not to keep patients alive indefinitely, it is to keep them alive so they can benefit from treatment. When that possibility is gone, so is the reason for artificial life support. That reasoning may be sound, but many people cannot bring themselves to accept it.

Issues that once seemed to be solved can crop up again when people least expect it. On January 11, 1983, twenty-five-year-old Nancy Cruzan was in a serious car accident. She was pronounced dead at the scene, but paramedics later revived her. Though her heart and lungs started working again, she never regained consciousness. Years later, her parents asked the hospital to disconnect her feeding tube.

When the hospital refused, Cruzan's parents took the matter to court. By December 1989, the case of *Cruzan* v. *Director, Missouri Department of Health* came before the United States Supreme Court.

On June 25, 1990, the court ruled that the state of Missouri could refuse to disconnect the tube because there was no "clear and convincing" evidence that Nancy herself would have wanted them to do so.

The case went back to court in Missouri when new evidence indicated that Nancy Cruzan would not have wanted to be kept alive by artificial means. On the court's decision, the hospital disconnected the tube. Nancy Cruzan died in December 1990, seven years after her accident.

## Terri Schiavo

In the year that Nancy Cruzan died, another young woman collapsed and went into a coma. The cause of Terri Schiavo's collapse has never been clear. It may have been a complication from an eating disorder.

Terri awakened after several weeks in a coma, but she did not become aware. She stared blankly ahead, reacting to nothing around her. Sometimes her eyes would move and she would make noises, but they had no purpose. Terri was not aware of her family, her environment, or even herself. The doctor diagnosed a persistent vegetative state that could not be cured or reversed.

**Artificial life support made it possible for a person to exist in a kind of twilight world, somewhere between life and death.**

Eight years later, Terri's husband, Michael, petitioned for a court order to remove her feeding tube and allow her to die. As Terri's court-appointed legal guardian, Michael had the right to do this. He also had a neurologist's report stating that eighty percent of Terri's upper brain had been destroyed. Her cerebral cortex showed no activity at all. This is the part of the brain that controls higher functions such as thought, reasoning, and memory.

Terri's parents, Bob and Mary Schindler, continued to hope that their daughter's condition would improve. They went to court to stop Michael from withdrawing the feeding tube. They claimed that Terri would want to live; Michael claimed that she would prefer to be allowed to die. The disagreements launched a series of legal battles that would last seven years and draw media attention from all over the world.

The controversy centered around the feeding tube. No matter how many experts said otherwise, taking away food and fluids seemed different from turning off a respirator. Terri did not need machines; her heart rate and respiration were fine. She only needed food and fluids, something that everyone needs to stay alive. The tube simply delivered the nourishment she needed in a form her body could tolerate.

Those who supported Michael Schiavo's position argued that artificial feeding is a form of treatment, especially since

Terri could neither feed herself nor swallow if food were placed in her mouth. Therefore, this treatment, like any other, could be discontinued if it became futile. The court agreed.

On March 18, 2005, doctors removed the feeding tube. Thirteen days later, on March 31, Terri Schiavo died. Autopsy results, released on June 15, 2005, confirmed that she had extensive brain damage and was blind.

Medical examiner Jon Thogmartin explained: "The brain weighed 615 grams, roughly half of the expected weight of a human brain. This damage was irreversible, and no amount of therapy or treatment would have regenerated [renewed] the massive loss of neurons."[5]

## Futility and Double Effect

Michael Schiavo's claim that his wife would not have wanted to live in her condition played an important role in the eventual decision. Medical futility was also a powerful argument. Numerous experts decided that Terri could not benefit from continued treatment; medicine had reached its limits.

In the brave new world of biotechnology, doctors often have to make tough decisions. Many rely upon the principle of futility or the principle of double effect to make those decisions.

"Futility" does not apply to people's lives or to their worth as human beings. It applies to treatments. Dr. Daniel Eisenberg defines a medically futile treatment as one "that will not reverse the condition to which it is being applied, even if successful."[6]

For example, continuing chemotherapy and radiation on a patient whose body is riddled with cancer would not only be futile but cruel. Reviving that patient if his or her heart should stop would not improve the chances of survival, lessen the pain, or prevent another cardiac or respiratory arrest.

There comes a time when the doctor, and sometimes the patient as well, may have to draw a line: this far and no further. Medical science has done all that it can do.

As Terri Schiavo's family engaged in a legal battle over her life, protesters urged the government to take action in the case.

The principle of double effect deals with another end-of-life issue: pain management. It recognizes that drugs can have both good and bad effects. Under certain conditions, a doctor can use the drug in spite of the bad effects.

Morphine is the perfect example of a double-effect drug. It can relieve severe pain that does not respond to other drugs. It can also kill.

Like all narcotics, morphine is highly addictive. It is closely related to the street drug heroin. Because of this, morphine is a "scheduled" drug, tightly regulated and monitored. Hospital pharmacies keep it under lock and key. Neighborhood drugstores do not carry it at all.

In ordinary cases, avoiding morphine may seem entirely sensible. However, it may not seem at all sensible to cancer patients with five or six months to live in unbearable pain. For these patients and their doctors, double effect can be a blessing.

When a patient is dying, relieving pain becomes the doctor's top priority. Because of the principle of double effect, the doctor can prescribe as much morphine as the patient needs, even in quantities that will shorten the patient's life. So long as the doctor intends only to control pain, he or she is not violating any law or ethical code. If the patient dies, that outcome becomes an unfortunate side effect of the good intent.

Not all medical ethicists agree with that. Some claim that the principle of double effect is "too clever for its own good."[7] They argue that double effect does not relieve the doctor of responsibility for his or her own actions. The doctor can foresee both the good and bad results and is therefore responsible for them. Also, they claim, not even the best of intentions can make death into a mere side effect of pain control.

## The Strange Career of Dr. Death

The debates over double effect are tame compared to the arguments over assisted suicide and euthanasia. Both involve doctors helping patients die. In assisted suicide, the doctor provides the means; the patient does the actual killing. In euthanasia, the doctor kills directly.

During a controversial public career, Dr. Jack Kevorkian practiced assisted suicide and eventually, active euthanasia. In the late 1980s, he became convinced that helping suffering people end their lives was both ethical and merciful. He began looking for suitable "clients."

In 1989, he found Janet Adkins, a fifty-four-year-old former music teacher. She had been diagnosed with Alzheimer's disease. This incurable condition ravages the brain, destroying memory and the ability to think.

Janet Adkins was still functioning fairly well when she met Jack Kevorkian. She could play tennis, though she could no longer figure out how to keep score. She was beginning to lose her ability to read music. She might have lived for many years, but she was afraid of waiting; she might lose the capacity to decide her own fate. In a videotaped interview with Dr. Kevorkian, Janet Adkins summed up her feelings in three words: "I've had enough."[8]

Dr. Kevorkian agreed. On June 4, 1990, he hooked Adkins to a "suicide machine." He started an intravenous (into-the-vein) drip of a harmless saltwater solution and gave Adkins a control device. With a push of a button, she sent poison into the intravenous tube, ending her life.

This death did not take place in a hospital room, with clean sheets and state-of-the-art equipment. It took place in Kevorkian's 1968 Volkswagen van, with a contraption he built from $30 worth of scrap parts.

Kevorkian did not try to keep the death of Janet Adkins a secret. He wanted all the publicity that he could get. Her assisted suicide was the beginning of his personal crusade for the right to die.

"Dr. Death," as Kevorkian came to be called, was charged

with murder in the death of Janet Adkins. The court dismissed the charges for lack of evidence.

As soon as he was free again, Kevorkian went back to work. He was not discriminating in his choices. Among his early clients were a fifty-eight-year-old woman who complained of pelvic pain and a thirty-nine-year-old woman who said she had multiple sclerosis. Autopsies found no evidence of disease in either woman.

Between 1990 and 1998, Kevorkian assisted in the deaths of over one hundred people.[9] Finally, in September 1998, "Dr. Death" went too far. Confronted with a client who had ALS and could not push the suicide button, Kevorkian went from assisted suicide to euthanasia. He not only gave fifty-three-year-old Thomas Youk a lethal injection, but videotaped the whole procedure. He then sent the tape to CBS Television's *60 Minutes.* On November 22, people all over the country watched Kevorkian end a human life.

This time, a jury found him guilty of murder in the second degree. In passing sentence of ten to twenty-five years in prison, Judge Jessica Cooper lectured Kevorkian: "You had the audacity to go on national television, show the world what you did and dare the legal system to stop you. Well, sir, consider yourself stopped."[10]

Kevorkian entered prison and disappeared from the limelight of the right-to-die movement. During his brief public career, he assisted in 130 suicides.[11] He claimed this number with evident pride, and people who favored assisted suicide admired him for it. Then Detroit-area medical examiner L. J. Dragovic released autopsy results for sixty-nine Kevorkian clients. Only seventeen of them had had a terminal illness. Five had no evidence of disease at all.[12]

Despite his mistakes and misjudgments, Kevorkian brought the right-to-die movement to public attention. This paved the way for less extreme activists. For example, in 1997 Oregon became the first state to allow doctor-assisted suicide.

## Graceful Exits

Oregon's Death With Dignity Act legalizes "ending life through the voluntary self-administration of lethal medications . . . prescribed by a physician for that purpose." It prohibits euthanasia, "where a physician or other person directly administers a medication to end another's life."[13]

Candidates for lethal prescriptions must be adult residents of Oregon who are mentally competent and have less than six

**Demonstrators urge the Supreme Court to uphold the Oregon law that allows doctors to help terminally ill patients end their lives.**

months to live. Meeting these qualifications is only the beginning of a careful, step-by-step process.

The patient must make three separate requests, two verbal and one written. The law requires two doctors to confirm the diagnosis and determine that the patient is not suffering from a psychological disorder, such as depression. The prescribing doctor must discuss alternatives to suicide, such as pain management and comfort care.

Comfort care begins with the acknowledgement that the person is dying and cannot be cured. Instead of continuing futile, or useless, treatment caregivers focus on symptom control. This often involves aggressive pain management, with narcotics if necessary.

The precautions built in to the evaluation system are rarely enough for people who believe that meddling with life and death is morally wrong. For people who consider themselves pro-life, the sanctity of human life is absolute; it applies to embryos created in vitro, to the very old and the very young, to people with disabilities, to those in a persistent vegetative state, and to those who are dying.

Right-to-die advocates recognize death as a natural part of the life cycle. Sooner or later, everyone dies. Assisted suicide, they say, gives dying patients some control over the time, place, and manner of death. To many people, this is both ethical and compassionate.

Hospice programs offer another choice. They create a nurturing environment in which patients can sort out their lives and prepare to end them with dignity. The National Hospice Association standards of care make this clear:

> Hospice affirms life. Hospice exists to provide support and care for persons in the last phases of incurable disease so that they might live as fully and as comfortably as possible. Hospice recognizes dying as a normal process whether or not resulting from disease. Hospice neither hastens nor postpones death. Hospice exists in the

hope and belief that, through appropriate care and the promotion of a caring community sensitive to their needs, patients and families may attain a degree of mental and spiritual preparation for death that is satisfactory to them."[14]

Preparing to die means striking a balance between the sanctity of life and the inevitability of death. The ethical questions that surround this process usually involve issues of control. Should human beings control their own living and dying? Should anyone have the right to decide when and how someone else dies? Should doctors assist suicides, and should they perform euthanasia?

These questions did not develop because of new technology. They are as old as humanity itself. The answers, however, are as new as artificial life support and advance directives. Bringing old ethical principles up to date with new biotechnology is likely to trigger changes in time-honored standards for dealing with life—and with death.

## Biotech on the Cutting Edge  7

Cutting-edge biotechnology is new, risky, and sometimes ethically troublesome. Much of it is experimental or in limited use, a situation that is likely to change in the twenty-first century. What was cutting edge in 2000 is likely to be commonplace in 2100.

The twenty-first century will see developments in fields such as stem cell research, cloning, and gene therapy. Brain implants may give people with disabilities more control over their lives. Genetic enhancement and life extension have already triggered debates about what it means to be human. These debates will not only continue, they will expand to include new issues and

The pace of this growth will have bioethicists scrambling to keep up with the latest developments. Artificial intelligence expert Ray Kurzweil explained how the sheer speed of change creates an issue of its own:

> The first technological steps—sharp edges, fire, the wheel—took tens of thousands of years. For people living in this era, there was little noticeable technological change in even a thousand years.
>
> By 1000 A.D., progress was much faster and a paradigm shift [a new worldview], required only a century or two. In the nineteenth century, we saw more technological change than in all the nine centuries preceding it. Then in the first twenty years of the twentieth century, we saw more advancement than in all of the nineteenth century. Now, paradigm shifts occur in only a few years time. The World Wide Web did not exist in anything like its present form just a few years ago; it didn't exist at all a decade ago [in 1991].[1]

Many people believe that gene therapy will be to medicine what the Internet is to communications. The term "gene therapy" includes two separate forms of treatment, linked chiefly by their focus on human genetic structure. Somatic therapy treats the human body on a cellular level. Germline therapy alters the genotype itself.

## Somatic Gene Therapy

Somatic gene therapy uses genes in much the same way that traditional medicine uses drugs or surgery: to treat a specific disease or abnormality. Because of this familiarity, it has not triggered major ethical controversies. Nobody protested in 1990 when doctors created functioning immune systems for two little girls with ADA deficiency.

Ten years later, a study of childhood immune disorders conducted in France won general approval. Immunologist Dr. Alain Fischer and his team treated ten babies for the X-linked form of severe combined immunodeficiency disorder.[2] This disorder is sometimes called "bubble-boy syndrome," after its most famous victim, a boy who spent his entire life inside a plastic isolation chamber, or "bubble."

By any name, it is a killer. Most victims die in infancy. Fischer's new treatment was risky, its outcome uncertain. It was also the last, best hope for these babies.

Fischer and his team took bone marrow cells from each child. They mixed these cells with viruses they had modified to carry healthy immune-system genes. When injected back into the child's bone marrow, the virus began copying and recopying the new genes, building a functioning immune system.

Former National Institutes of Health (NIH) researcher Dr. R. Michael Blaese hailed Fischer's accomplishment. He called it "the first example in any disease where gene therapy could be a fully successful treatment" and remarked that "You can't distinguish these patients from normal."[3]

The NIH supported somatic therapy as "a logical and natural" way of applying "biomedical science to medicine." The agency further stated that somatic therapy "offers extraordinary potential . . . for the management of human disease, including inherited and acquired disorders, cancer, and AIDS."[4]

In the same report, the NIH warned: "Significant problems remain in all basic [parts] of gene therapy."[5] Those significant problems turned out to include leukemia for two of the young patients.[6]

Fischer and his team shut down the study; researchers all over the world halted similar projects. Both ethics and sound research procedures demanded nothing less.

Despite the setback, Fischer's team did not give up on gene therapy. Their search for answers led them to gene LM02, a known cause of leukemia. Something in the treatment had switched it on, but only for two of the children.

The researchers began by examining the differences between the children who got leukemia and those who did not. They found that the stricken babies were the youngest of the group;

one was three months old, the other only one month. The rest were at least six months old. They also discovered that the two leukemia victims had received more corrected cells than the other children.

The team adjusted the treatment protocols and, in June 2004, resumed the study. Other researchers followed suit. Donald Kohn, lead researcher for one of the U.S. trials, said: "We're moving forward. . . . No therapy is without risk, and now that we've had time to look back, we realize that this therapy even with the risk may be better than the current treatment."[7]

## Germline Therapy and Embryo Selection

Germline therapy would not just treat a particular person with a particular disease; it would change the genotype—the genetic structure—of days-old embryos. The resulting baby would pass on the changes to its descendants. In the early twenty-first century, the technology for germline therapy does not yet exist.

Some people would like to keep it that way. Even if humankind had the knowledge to shape its own evolution, it might not have the wisdom to make the right choices. Genes interact with one another. Adding new genes or removing mutated ones might trigger dangerous or even deadly changes.

Opponents of germline technology claim that there is a safer way to ensure a child's genetic health: testing embryos for genetic defects before they are implanted and then selecting the best embryos to implant. People who favor testing point out that it does not change the embryos in any way, nor does it involve genetic manipulation. Embryos would still be the natural product of the parents' DNA, with nothing changed, nothing added, and nothing taken away. Because of this, many consider screening a useful and less risky alternative to genetic engineering.

Not everyone agrees. Some argue that screening and embryo selection could upset the natural balance by imposing

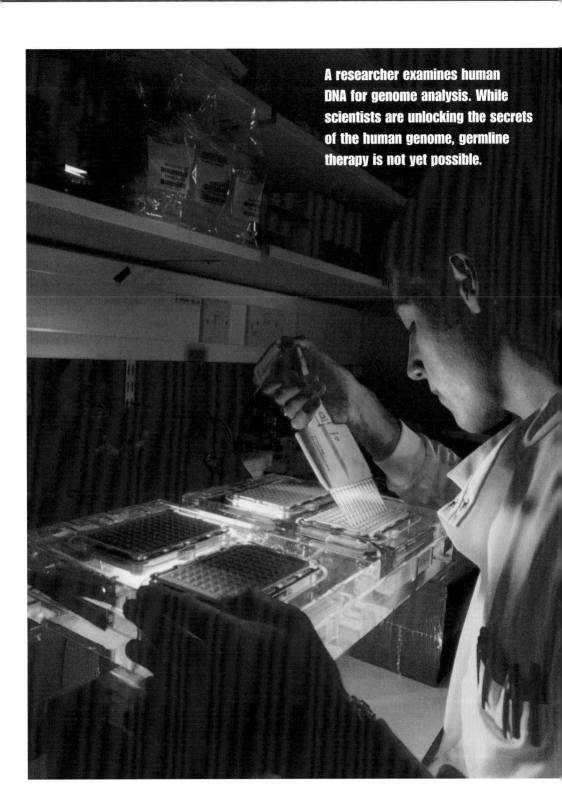

A researcher examines human DNA for genome analysis. While scientists are unlocking the secrets of the human genome, germline therapy is not yet possible.

social values on a fundamental biological process. For example, in cultures that value males over females, gender selection might create an imbalance that would eventually lower the birth rate and disrupt the society.

Other opponents of selection are concerned about the process itself. It would involve creating many embryos, then discarding those that are not selected. People who consider embryos human life reject this on moral grounds. Antiabortionists worry that more testing will lead to more abortions.

At present, that may be true; tests can detect serious abnormalities that medicine cannot cure. For example, genetic conditions such as Down syndrome, Tay-Sachs disease, or sickle-cell anemia create a heartbreaking choice: abort the fetus or allow it to be born with serious defects.

Many prospective parents with known genetic defects look at the situation differently. Without testing, they would not have children for fear of passing on a deadly disease or condition. Those who consider abortion unethical face especially painful choices. If they do not test, they risk passing on a serious genetic defect. If they do test, they could be forced to choose between bringing a severely disabled child into the world or violating their own moral code.

Many scientists contend that germline intervention will one day offer another choice: correct the genotype by replacing abnormal genes with healthy ones. Each germline correction would eliminate the flaw from an entire genetic line. In time, diseases like sickle-cell anemia and Tay-Sachs disease might well disappear from the human genome.

In spite of such possibilities, many people resist altering the human gene pool. Some call it "playing God," and worry that a single misjudgment could bring disaster.

Some argue that it is impossible to know the consequences of changing the genetic pool. An apparently harmful gene might play a necessary role in the overall genetic balance. Many people are simply not willing to take such a risk. Others believe that the risk is justified by the potential rewards. James Watson, codiscoverer of DNA structure, counts himself among this group. At a symposium in 1998, he spoke against what he called the "sanctity" of the gene pool:

> I just can't indicate how silly I think [this idea] is. I mean, sure, we have great respect for the human species. We like each other. We'd like to be better, and we take great pleasure in achievements by other people. But evolution can be . . . cruel, and to say that we've got a perfect genome . . . and there's some sanctity to it . . . [is] utter silliness. What we want to do is treat other people the way that maximizes the common good of the human species. And that's about all we can do.[8]

Opponents counter with a two-part question: What is the common good, and who will have the right to decide? They point to problems with "selective breeding" as it has been practiced for generations. Long before humankind had any idea about the mechanisms of heredity, people tried to shape the characteristics of the offspring by selecting parents with specific, desirable characteristics. This resulted in a great deal of inbreeding—the mating of closely related individuals.

For example, European royalty jealously guarded the "purity" of its bloodlines. A handful of royal families intermarried with one another, passing on the gene for hemophilia, a hereditary disease in which blood does not clot normally. Even small injuries can produce uncontrolled bleeding.

The problem appears to have begun with Queen Victoria of England, who passed the gene through the royal houses of Europe. Women are carriers of the disease. They do not develop it themselves (unless they are the daughters of a hemophiliac and a carrier), but pass it to male offspring. Victoria's daughters married into the courts of Spain, Germany, and Russia and bore sons with hemophilia. It was so common during the late nineteenth century that many called it "the royal disease."[9]

## The Promise and the Problems of Stem Cells

Stem cell technology raises as many ethical issues as germline manipulation. Stem cells are like no other cells in the body. Unlike blood cells, or heart cells, or any other kind of cells, they have not developed a specific function of their own. British physician Dr. Robert Marcus called them "the basic seed cells of the body" and noted that they "turn into the mature cells that [form] all the organs and tissues in the body . . . in the same way that seeds turn into flowers."[10]

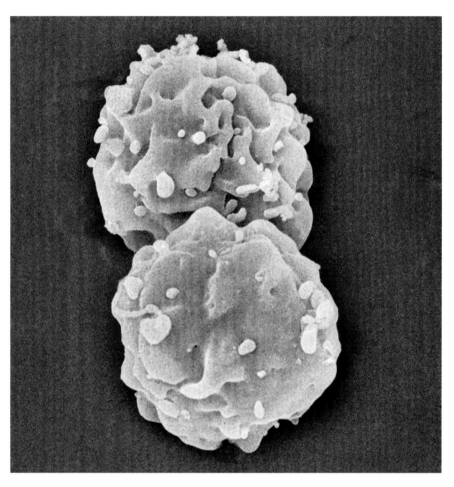

**Research on human embryonic stem cells, pictured here, is controversial, since five- to six-day-old embryos are destroyed in the process.**

The most adaptable "seeds" come from five- to six-day-old embryos. These cells can rebuild damaged tissue by replacing abnormal or diseased cells with healthy new ones. This technology might cure conditions like multiple sclerosis, Alzheimer's disease, Parkinson's disease, and even spinal cord injuries.

Almost no one has an ethical problem about treating once-incurable diseases. Disagreements focus on the origin of the cells. People who believe that life begins with conception oppose embryonic stem cell research on moral grounds. Those who believe that life begins at birth argue the opposite point of view—that it would be immoral to ignore such promising technology. Actor Christopher Reeve of *Superman* fame took this position when he testified before a Senate subcommittee on April 26, 2000. Reeve had become an outspoken activist for embryonic stem cell research after a 1995 accident left him paralyzed from the neck down.

In his appeal to the subcommittee, he proposed using embryos left over from fertility treatments. "Why has the use of discarded embryos for research suddenly become such an issue? Is it more ethical for a woman to donate unused embryos that will never become human beings, or to let them be tossed away like so much garbage when they could help save thousands of lives?"[11]

Reeve's testimony attracted interest in stem cell research and the ethical issues surrounding it. This stimulated public discussion, but it did not answer the underlying question: When does human life begin?

The issue dragged through the House of Representatives and the Senate. Bioethicists, clergy, doctors, and health care activists gave their opinions. People signed petitions and wrote letters.

Christopher Reeve died on October 10, 2004, at the age of fifty-two. Four and a half years had passed since his testimony to the Senate. The fundamental issues surrounding embryonic stem cell research remained unresolved.

## Cloning: Building People, Saving Lives

Like stem cell research, cloning is both promising and controversial. A clone is an exact genetic copy of a living—or once-living—organism: perhaps a plant, an animal, or even a human being. Though the process of cloning in the laboratory is cutting-edge biotechnology, the existence of clones is as old as humankind itself, since identical twins are exact genetic copies of one another.

There are two forms of cloning: reproductive and therapeutic. Though their methods are similar, their goals are not. Reproductive cloning would create a new individual from the DNA of a single donor. Therapeutic cloning would produce genetically matched body parts to replace malfunctioning ones.

Reproductive cloning is by far the more controversial of the two. Some people reject it out of hand for religious or philosophical reasons. Others worry about its impact on society: Would clones be fully human, or have a soul? How would their existence affect family relationships?

A family tree that includes clones would present some interesting challenges. For example, a DNA donor would not be the cloned child's parent in the usual sense of the word. Genetically, the two would be more like identical twins who just happened to be born a generation apart.

Until 1997, these questions did not seem particularly urgent. Cloning was at best a remote possibility, more science fiction than science fact. Then on February 22, 1997, in Scotland, two scientists introduced the world to a six-month-old lamb named Dolly. She was the first mammal to be cloned from the cells of an adult donor.

Dolly made headlines all over the world. Cloning did not seem like science fiction anymore. If scientists could clone a sheep, sooner or later they would figure out how to clone a human being.

The very idea horrifies social and religious conservatives who see themselves locked in a struggle to protect traditional values. Of all the new and morally disturbing developments in biotechnology, nothing is quite so unsettling as using science to create human life.

Many call for strict laws against the cloning of human beings. They fear that without such laws, cloning might one day run rampant, changing the very nature of the human race.

Some consider this an overreaction. Biologist Daniel Koshland, Jr., suggests that reproductive cloning would not threaten the human race or the social order: "Individuals . . . are usually interested in establishing a life record that is not only considerable, but also unique. . . . My guess is that people's demands for self-cloning will be very low."

Therefore, Koshland sees no need to make laws against cloning. At a symposium on human germline engineering, he illustrated his point with a touch of humor:

> Outlawing the cloning of one's self seems to me a little like outlawing ballooning around the world. You know, balloons may land in the

**The first cloned cat, "cc" (for "carbon copy"), was born in 2001; she is shown with her surrogate mother. Cloning appeared to be a remote possibility until 1997, when the first mammal was cloned.**

back yard now and then and do some damage, but the frequency of ballooning around the world really doesn't demand that we pass a law against ballooning around the world."[12]

Other scientists have expressed similar views, but the general public is not convinced. Many people do not share the opinion that reproductive cloning will prove to be harmless. Despite the controversy, there is no law against cloning. The debate has focused on government funding of cloning projects.

The backlash against reproductive cloning has affected attitudes toward therapeutic cloning, or somatic cell nuclear transfer, as it is more properly called. This process—still theoretical at this point—would begin with an embryo, cloned from a subject's DNA and grown to the point that it would produce stem cells. Scientists would stimulate these stem cells to grow into tissues or organs, which would then be transplanted into the patient. The process of "harvesting" stem cells would destroy the embryo, and this fact is at the heart of the ethical debate surrounding stem cell research.

The benefits of such a procedure would be dazzling. People would no longer die waiting for suitable organs, and shortages would become a thing of the past. So would tissue rejection; the body's immune system would "read" the new implant as if it were the original. Patients would not have to take expensive antirejection drugs for the rest of their lives.

Somatic cell transfer could grow a new heart, lung, or liver. It could even regrow nerve tissue to treat neurological diseases like Parkinson's, multiple sclerosis, and Alzheimer's.

No one objects to saving lives, or to making transplants safe and readily available. The ethical issues revolve around the cloned embryo. Some worry that it might be misused to create a person instead of a body part. Some object to creating an embryo for the sole purpose of harvesting its stem cells.

Most supporters of somatic cell transfer are interested in its medical uses. For example, Christopher Reeve lobbied for this limited use of cloning technology as part of his argument for stem cell research.

In the midst of the controversy about embryonic stem cells, researchers have made an exciting discovery: Undifferentiated cells still exist in adults. They are mixed in with ordinary cells, and apparently lie dormant, or inactive, until they are needed to fight disease or rebuild damaged tissue.

With the proper techniques, scientists may be able to locate and harvest adult stem cells without damage to the donor. Those cells could then be copied, or cloned, so that a relative few of them could produce new cells as they are needed. According to the National Institutes of Health, researchers have already had some success in getting adult stem cells to replace injured tissue in a living animal.[13]

## The Quest for Longer Life

The prospect of grown-to-order body parts and cells that can adapt to different functions is exciting to people who dream of extending the human life span. Some speculate about achieving immortality, with a body and mind that can be rebuilt as necessary and function indefinitely.

For most people, speculation about immortality is just that: speculation. Human beings and everything else that lives are programmed to die. It is part of the natural life cycle. Biologist Michael West wants to change that cycle. Aging, he says, "is a disease that is killing everyone."[14]

Texas oilman Miller Quarles liked the idea of treating aging as a disease to be cured. In 1992, he founded an organization called the Cure Old Age Disease Society and helped to fund Michael West's research on aging.

By 2000, immortality was nowhere in sight, but biotechnology was making headway in extending the human life span. The average life expectancy for a baby born in 2000 was seventy-seven years; for one born in 1900, it was only forty-eight years.[15]

What is now considered cutting-edge biotechnology is too new to have been a major factor in shaping these figures. Reduced infant mortality rates and improved public health procedures accounted for much of the progress in the twentieth century. In 1900, the infant mortality rate was 165 per 1,000; by 1997, it was only 7 per 1,000.[16] This obviously had a tremendous impact on average life expectancy. As people lived longer, healthier lives, some began wondering about the upper limit. How long was long enough?

Longevity researchers talk about breakthroughs that will allow life spans of five hundred or even a thousand years.[17] A few dare to talk about immortality.

Cell biologist Leonard Hayflick dismissed such predictions out of hand. He claimed that curing everything from Alzheimer's and Parkinson's diseases to stroke, cancer, diabetes, and hepatitis would only add about fifteen years to average life expectancy. He predicted that the average life span would not rise above ninety—at least not in the twenty-first century.

Hayflick's opinion cannot be ignored. He confronted mortality in a petri dish and transformed cellular science. Cells grow by dividing; one cell splits to make two; both daughter cells split, and so the process goes. In 1962, Hayflick discovered that normal cells in a nutrient solution would divide, or grow, about fifty times. Then they simply stopped: "They didn't die immediately." said Hayflick. "In fact, they will stay that way for a year or more, without dividing [growing]. They'll [function] but they won't divide."[18]

The discovery became known as the "Hayflick limit." It demonstrated that cells are mortal; when they stop dividing, they start aging. In time they die. Death is programmed into the human genome as a natural part of the life cycle.

Longevity researchers redirected their efforts to find a way around the Hayflick limit. It was a daunting task, looking for the biological clock that triggers the process of aging.

In time, researchers began examining peculiar strands of DNA that are a part of both ends of every chromosome, like plastic caps on a shoestring. Telomeres, as these genetic "caps" are called, have an interesting characteristic: they shorten every time the cell divides.

In 1990, biochemist Calvin Harley and his research team showed that telomere shortening is linked to cellular aging. When the telomeres become too short, cells stop dividing; senescence, or aging, begins.

Harley's team also found a gene that produces a protein called telomerase. It made short telomeres grow and old cells divide. In the process, it broke an evolutionary barrier. Telomere shortening and cellular aging is a natural defense against the uncontrolled cell growth that produces cancer.

Cancer cells survive and spread by somehow activating telomerase. It makes them effectively immortal, because they never stop dividing. Nothing illustrates this characteristic better than the case of Henrietta Lacks. In 1951, Lacks was diagnosed with cancer; eight months later she died. Her doctor gave some of the cancer cells to Johns Hopkins University, for use in research. They named the strain HeLa, after the first letters in Lacks's first and last names. The cells thrived, growing so well in cultures that they were shipped to research centers all over the world. The HeLa strain has survived into the twenty-first century.

## The Ethics of Immortality

At some time in the history of humankind, people realized that everybody dies and that death is permanent. Since that time, they have sought a way to escape death. Some believe that twenty-first century biotechnology will find that way. Others claim that nothing can find it for the simple reason that it does not exist; death is part of the natural order of existence. Still others focus on the social and ethical issues of extreme

**Some people view aging as a disease to be cured, while others see it as a natural part of life. If the life span were extended, it would cause major changes in society.**

longevity. Instead of asking what *can* be done, they ask what *should* be done.

That turns out to be a surprisingly difficult question to answer. At present, most scientists are not looking for the secret of immortality. They are studying the mechanisms of aging, and seeking cures for age-related conditions such as Alzheimer's disease, heart disease, and stroke.

It would be difficult for anyone to criticize these goals. However, curing disease will lengthen life expectancy. The two cannot be separated. That fact creates an ethical dilemma: continue aging research and ignore the longevity issue, or curtail research and ignore the suffering of real people in the here-and-now.

Increases in life expectancy could create a whole new set of social problems. For example, if people routinely lived for 150 to 200 years, the elderly would soon outnumber all other age groups. They would control great wealth and political power.

Should life span outstrip medical science, diseases of old age could make society "resemble a giant nursing home," in the words of political economist Francis Fukuyama. He offers a worst-case scenario "in which people routinely live to be 150 but spend the last fifty years in a state of childlike dependence on caretakers."[19]

Under circumstances such as these, life extension would take a hefty toll on society. Legions of frail elderly could swamp social service and health care facilities. Economies could founder under the burden of caring for so many. Some people believe that the situation could be even worse if humankind achieved virtual immortality. A race of immortals would destroy the present social order as well as the natural rhythms of birth and death, growth and decline. Young people would have an especially difficult time finding a place for themselves in society.

Science writer Charles C. Mann commented on the plight of the young in a society of the old:

> From religion to real estate, from pensions to parent-child dynamics, almost every aspect of society is based on the orderly succession of generations. Every quarter century or so children take over from their parents—a transition as fundamental to human existence as the rotation of the planet around its axis.[20]

Unimaginably old people would control economic and political power, their interests, needs, and attitudes shaping entire cultures. Their ethics would dictate cultural values. In time, the sameness in this society of the old could lead to social stagnation.

In more optimistic views, immortality could lead to wisdom. The threat of social stagnation could spur some of these new humans to break the mold, to investigate new dimensions of existence, colonize other planets, or simply change identity and environment from time to time to avoid boredom.

People who desire immortality and those who fear it have one thing in common: both must base their decisions on incomplete information. This is nothing new. It has been happening ever since human beings climbed down from the trees and walked on two legs through the African savanna. Information is always incomplete, and decisions can always lead to unexpected results.

## Ethics and Uncertainty

Ethics, bioethics included, is not an exact science. It evolves along with social institutions, as a way of ordering human relationships. Different walks of life have their special ethical codes. Doctors and lawyers swear allegiance to an ethical system, police officers promise to protect and to serve, clergy teach ethics according to the tenets of their particular religion. Bioethicists have confronted everything from abortion and birth defects to genetic engineering, assisted suicide, and medical care for the very old.

Each scientific or technological innovation seems to bring its particular ethical issues. Doctors can keep brain-dead people alive indefinitely; should they? Researchers are working towards control of DNA, the very mechanism of heredity. How far can they go without doing harm?

There are no hard-and-fast answers to such questions, and no guarantees against mistakes or misunderstandings. However, ethical codes do not exist to create perfection; they exist to provide grounding and guidance in the face of new challenges.

From the Hippocratic oath to ELSI, the system is imperfect, but it is nonetheless important. It offers the best chance to keep the quest for scientific knowledge on a human scale and ensure that biotechnology serves humankind rather than the other way around.

# Chapter Notes

**Chapter 1**    The Biotech Revolution

1. Michael Burnham and Rod Mitchell, "Bioethics—An Introduction," *Woodrow Wilson Biology Institute*, 1992, <http://www.woodrow.org/teachers/bi/1992/bioethics_intro.html> (February 6, 2006).

2. "Hippocratic oath," n.d., <http://www.hal-pc.org/~ollie/hippocratic.oath.html> (February 6, 2006).

3. Ibid.

4. "The Nuremberg Code," *Chicago State University*, n.d., <http://www.csu.edu.au/learning/ncgr/gpi/odyssey/privacy/NurCode.html> (February 6, 2006).

5. "International Consortium Completes Human Genome Project: All Goals Achieved; New Vision for Genome Research Unveiled," *Whitehead Institute/MIT Center for Genome Research*, April 14, 2003, <http://www.wi.mit.edu/news/archives/2003/el_0414.html> (February 25, 2006).

6. "The Human Genome Project Completion: Frequently Asked Questions," *National Human Genome Research Institute*, news release, 2003, <http://www.genome.gov/11006943> (June 27, 2006).

7. Bill McKibben, *Enough: Staying Human in an Engineered Age* (New York: Henry Holt and Company, 2003), p. xii.

8. "Twenty Questions About DNA Sequencing (And the Answers)," National Human Genome Research Institute, n.d., <http://www.dur.ac.uk/biological.sciences/Bioinformatics/twenty_questions_about_DNA.htm> (February 16, 2005).

**Chapter 2**    Research and Development

1. Jan Goodwin, "The Family Curse," *Reader's Digest*, March 2005, p. 112.

2. People for the Ethical Treatment of Animals, "PETA Mission Statement," <http://www.peta.org/about/> (March 21, 2005).

3. Patrick M. Cleveland, Ph.D., "Animal Rights; Pro and Con," *The*

*Pet Professor*, December 9, 1992, <http://www.thepetprofessor. com/articles/article.aspx?id=491> (February 5, 2006).

4. "Sour legacy of Tuskegee syphilis study lingers," *CNN*, May 16, 1997, <http://www.cnn.com/HEALTH/9705/16/nfm.tuskegee> (March 20, 2005).

5. "Remembering Tuskegee," *National Public Radio*, July 25, 2002, <http://www.npr.org/programs/morning/features/2002/jul/ tuskegee> (March 24, 2005).

6. "Former Willowbrook Resident Speaks Out," *WABC-TV*, February 7, 2005. <http://www.abclocal.go.com/wabc/news/ investigators/print_wabc_020705_investigatorsstory_willowbrook. html> (March 20, 2005).

7. "Shocking New Willowbrook Legacy," *WABC-TV*, February 1, 2005, <http://abclocal.go.com/wabc/news/ investigators/wabc_020105_investigatorsstory_willowbrook.html>

8. Ibid.

9. Tony Levene, "Ethical Investment," *UK Guardian*, February 22, 1999, <http://www.intekom.com/tm_info/rw90223.htm#02> (May 12, 2005).

## Chapter 3   Public Health: The Good of the Many

1. "Fluoridation/Fluoride: Toxic Chemicals in Your Water," *Holistic Healing Web Page*, n.d., <http://www.holisticmed.com/fluoride/> (March 12, 2005).

2. American Academy of Family Physicians, "Fluoridation of Public Water Supplies," Policy Statement, 2005, <http://www.aafp.org/ x1585.xml?printxml> (March 12, 2005).

3. "The History of AIDS and ARC," *LSU Law Center's Medical and Public Health Site*, n.d., <http://biotech.law.lsu.edu/Books/lbb/ x590.htm> (April 4, 2005).

4. "So Little Time: An AIDS History," *Aids Education Global Information System*, n.d., <http://www.aegis.com/topics/timeline/ default.asp> (April 2, 2005).

5. "United States HIV & AIDS Statistics Summary," *Avert.org*, n.d., <http://www.avert.org/statsum.htm> (April 7, 2005).

6. "World HIV & AIDS Statistics," *Avert.org*, n.d., <http://www.avert.org/worldstats.htm> (April 7, 2005).

7. Tom Paulson, "1918 killer flu virus to be tested in UW lab," *Seattle Post-Intelligencer*, September 18, 2004, <http://seattlepi. nwsource.com/health/191418_flu18.html> (February 20, 2006).

8. Ibid.

9. Tony Levene, "Ethical Investment," *UK Guardian*, February 20, 1999, <http://home.intekom.com/tm_info/rw90223.htm#02> (May 12, 2005).

10. Karl A. Thiel, "Seeds in the Wind: For Monsanto, Patent Protection Stirs Controversy," *Biospace*, n.d., <http://www. biospace.com/articles/120699_print.cfm> (April 11, 2005).

11. "Schmeiser Decision Causes Uproar Around the World," *Canadian NewsWire*, May 21, 2004, <http://www.mindfully.org/GE/ 2004/Schmeiser-Uproar-World21may04.htm> (April 12, 2005).

12. Ibid.

13. "Quotes from some members of the Independent Science Panel on GM," *ISP*, n.d., <http://www.indsp.org/quotes.php> (February 10, 2006).

14. Dr. Norman Bourlag, "We Need Biotech to Feed the World," editorial, *Wall Street Journal*, December 6, 2000, <http://www. europabio.org/documents/140404/ne_140404_t_7.htm> (February 12, 2006).

**Chapter 4**   Ethics at the Beginning of Life

1. David Allyn, "The Pill: A Prescription for Equality, Part 3," *eNotAlone*, 2000, <http://www. enotalone.com/article/3961.html> (February 22, 2006).

2. James M. Wallace, "Anti-abortion violence negates pro-life goals," Letter to the Editor, *News & Record* (Greensboro, N.C.), October 11, 1998.

3. Gregory E. Pence, *Classic Cases in Medical Ethics*, 3rd ed. (New York: McGraw-Hill Higher Education, 2000), p. 122.

4. "In Vitro Success Rate Doubles," *CBSNEWS.com*, July 24, 2003,

<http://www.cbsnews.com/stories/2003/07/24/tech/main565014. shtml> (April 15, 2005).

5. "In Vitro Fertilization," *WebMD*, September 2003, <http://my. webmd.com/content/article/73/87998?z=3074_00000_1043_ 00_04> (April 28, 2005).

6. "'World's oldest mum' defends her decision," *MSNBC*, January 18, 2005, <http://msnbc.msn.com/id/6839463/> (April 20, 2005).

7. Kyle R. Wood, "Family Law: In the Matter of Baby M.," 109 N.J. 396 (1988) University of Washington School of Law, <http://www. kylewood.com/familylaw/babym.htm> (February 9, 2006).

8. Pence, p. 153.

9. Ibid., pp. 154–155.

10. Carol Levine, *Taking Sides: Clashing Views on Controversial Bioethical Issues*, 6th ed. (Guilford, Conn.: The Duskin Publishing Group, 1995), p. 68.

11. Ibid., pp. 68–69.

12. U.S. Food and Drug Administration, "New Drug Label Spells It Out Simply," *FDA Consumer Magazine*, July–August 1999, <http://www.pueblo.gsa.gov/cic_text/health/newdrug-label/499_ otc.html> (February 12, 2006).

**Chapter 5**    Allocating Medical Resources

1. Robert Derlet, M.D., "Triage," *Emedicine*, September 14, 2004, <http://www.emedicine.com/emerg/topic670.htm> (April 28, 2005).

2. "Babies Born Preterm Cost Businesses Big Money; Hospital Charges Estimated at $7.4 Billion Annually," *March of Dimes News Desk*, March 28, 2005, <http://www.marchofdimes.com/aboutus/ 14458_15365.asp> (May 29, 2005).

3. Jan L. Warner and Jan Collins, "Advance Directives and Medicare," *NextSteps*, n.d., <http://www.lifemanagement.com/ nsa1.1.2067> (May 30, 2005).

4. Carol Levine, *Taking Sides: Clashing Views on Controversial Bioethical Issues*, 6th ed. (Guilford, Conn.: The Duskin Publishing Group, 1995), p. 303.

5. Daniel Callahan, "Conservative, Liberals, and Medical Progress," *The New Atlantis*, Fall 2005, <http://www.thenewatlantis.com/archive/10/callahan.htm> (February 10, 2006).

6. "Insight: Life After Death," *Hinduism Today*, September 1999, <http://www.hinduismtoday.com/archives/1999/9/1999-9-11.shtml> (February 13, 2006).

7. Dr. John Fung, "Ethics of Transplantation," Thomas E. Starzl Transplantation Institute, <http://www.sti.upmc.edu/STI_Patient_web/sti/text/faq.asp#ethics> (April 29, 2005).

8. "Kidney Pre-Transplantation," *Novartis Transplant*, 2002, <http://www.novartis-transplant.com/public/pre_kidney/donation_process.html> (April 30, 2005).

9. "U.S. Transplantation Data," United Network for Organ Sharing, <http://www.unos.org/data/default.asp?displayType=usData> (May 3, 2005).

10. Bryan Robinson, "Death Row Privilege," *ABCNews.com*, May 28, 2004, <http://www.liberty-page.com/issues/healthcare/organs/deathrow.html> (May 1, 2005).

11. Victoria Colliver, "Excessive medical expenses: Study finds that half of health care dollars are wasted," *SFGate.com*, February 9, 2005, <http://www.sfgate.com/cgi-bin/article.cgi?f=/c/a/2005/02/09/BUG7RB7VEM1.DTL>

12. Sheila McLean, *Old Law, New Medicine: Medical Ethics and Human Rights* (London: Pandora Press, 1999), p. 175.

13. Ahmedin Jemal, et al. "Cancer Statistics, January, 2005," *CA: A Cancer Journal for Clinicians*, 2005, <http://caonline.amcancersoc.org/cgi/content/abstract/55/1/10> (May 10, 2005).

**Chapter 6**   Ethics at the End of Life

1. "Deciding about CPR Do Not Resuscitate Orders (DNR): A Guide for Patients and Families," State of New York Department of Health, <http://www.health.state.ny.us/nysdoh/ems/pdf/doh3474.pdf> (May 15, 2005).

2. "Real survival rates from CPR can't compete with TV doctors' success," *CBC Health & Science News*, August 20, 2002, <http://

www.cbc.ca/story/science/national/2002/08/20/cpr020820.html>
(May 14, 2005).

3. Mark H. Ebell, "Practical guidelines for do-not-resuscitate orders," *American Family Physician*, November 1, 1994, <http://www.findarticles.com/p/articles/mi_m3225/is_n6_v50/ai_15863864> (May 12, 2005).

4. Bob Lane, "Euthanasia," 2005, <http://www.mala.bc.ca/www/ipp/euthanas.htm> (February 14, 2006).

5. "Schiavo State Was Irreversible," *CBS News*, June 15, 2005, <http://www.cbsnews.com/stories/2005/06/14/national/main7019 09.shtml> (June 16, 2005).

6. Daniel Eisenberg, M.D., "Should Terri Schiavo Live or Die?" *Society Today*, February 21, 2005, <http://www.aish.com/society Work/sciencenature/Should_Terri_Schiavo_Live_or_Die$.asp> (May 18, 2005).

7. "The Doctrine of Double Effect," *BBC—Religion & Ethics— Euthanasia*, n.d., <http://www.bbc.co.uk/print//religion/ethics/euthanasia/euth_double_effect.shtml> (May 14, 2005).

8. Walter Goodman, "Review/Television; The Words That Inspired Dr. Kevorkian's Actions." *New York Times*, April 5, 1994, <http://query.nytimes.com/gst/fullpage.html?res=9904EEDF1E3F F936A35757C0A962958260> (February 16, 2006).

9. "Dr. Jack Kevorkian and Cases of Euthanasia in Oakland County, Michigan, 1990–1998," *New England Journal of Medicine*, 343:1735–1736.

10. Justin Hyde, "Kevorkian sentenced," *Seacoastonline.com*, April 14, 1999, <http://www.seacoastonline.com/1999news/4_14_w2.htm> (May 30, 2005).

11. Ibid.

12. "More women than men sought Kevorkian's help," *Berkeley Daily Planet*, December 8, 2000, <http://www.berkeleydaily.org/article.cfm?archiveDate=12-08-00&storyID=2561> (June 6, 2005).

13. "Oregon's Death with Dignity Act: The First Year's Experience," Department of Human Resources, Oregon Health Division, Center for Disease Prevention and Epidemiology, February 18,

1999, p. 1, <http://egov.oregon.gov/DHS/ph/pas/docs/year1.pdf> (June 5, 2005).

14. National Hospice Organization, "Standards of a Hospice Program of Care," August 15, 2001, <http://www.hospice-america.org/home.html> (June 10, 2005).

## Chapter 7    Biotech on the Cutting Edge

1. Ray Kurzweil, "The Law of Accelerating Returns," *KurzweilAI.net*, March 7, 2001, <http://www.kurzweilai.net/articles/art0134.html?printable=1> (June 15, 2005).

2. Laura Bonetta, "Lukemia case triggers tighter gene-therapy controls," *Nature Medicine*, 2002, <http://www.nature.com/nm/journal/v8/n11/full/nm1102-1189.html;jsessionid=595DB7AF243DF63E4000EDA3D19C27F3#top> (June 20, 2005).

3. Gina Kolata, "Scientists Report First Success of Gene Therapy," *New York Times*, April 28, 2000, p. 1.

4. Stuart H. Orkin and Arno G. Moluisky, "Report and Recommendations of the Panel to Assess the NIH Investment in Research on Gene Therapy," *National Institutes of Health*, December 7, 1995, <http://www.nih.gov/news/panelrep.html> (June 20, 2005).

5. Ibid.

6. Eliot Marshall, "Gene Therapy: Second Child in French Trial Is Found to Have Leukemia," *Science*, vol. 299, no. 5605, January 17, 2003, p. 320.

7. Erika Check, "Gene therapists hopeful as trials resume with childhood disease," *news@nature.com*, 2004, <http://www.nature.com/news/2004/040607/pf/429587a_pf.html> (June 26, 2005).

8. "Engineering the Human Germline Symposium: Summary Report, June 1998," <http://www.ess.ucla.edu/huge/report.html> (June 29, 2005).

9. "History," *Hemophilia Research Today: Genetics, Causes, Symptoms, Blood Transfusion*, 2005–2006, <http://hemophilia.researchtoday.net/about-hemophilia.htm> (February 19, 2006).

10. Erica Heilman, "Keeping Pace with the News: Stem Cells

Simplified," *ABC News*, August 16, 2002, <http://www.healthology.com/printer_friendlyAR.asp?b=rxlist&f=xmlpressfeed&c=stemcell_anniversary&spg=SCH> (August 31, 2004).

11. "Christopher Reeve on Stem Cell Research," *Your Congress.com*, n.d., <http://www.yourcongress.com/ViewArticle.asp?article_id=225> (June 30, 2005).

12. "Engineering the Human Germline Symposium: Summary Report, June, 1998."

13. National Institutes of Health, "Stem Cell Information," August 12, 2005, <http://stemcells.nih.gov/info/basics/basics4.asp> (February 19, 2006).

14. Bill McKibben, *Enough: Staying Human in an Engineered Age* (New York: Henry Holt and Company, 2003), p. 146.

15. "Life Expectancy," U.S. Centers for Disease Control, National Institute on Aging, April 4, 2005, <http://tristatehealthsystem.client.web-health.com/web-health/topics/GeneralHealth/generalhealthsub/generalhealth/lifestyle/Death/life_expectancy.html> (June 9, 2005).

16. "Infant Mortality and Life Expectancy," *The First Measured Century*, n.d., <http://www.pbs.org/fmc/timeline/dmortality.htm> (February 19, 2006).

17. Stephen S. Hall, *Merchants of Immortality: Chasing the Dream of Human Life Extension* (Boston: Houghton Mifflin Company, 2003), p. 345.

18. Ibid., p. 24.

19. Francis Fukuyama, *Our Posthuman Future: Consequences of the Biotechnology Revolution* (New York: Farrar, Straus and Giroux, 2002), pp. 67, 69.

20. Charles C. Mann, "The Coming Death Shortage: Why the longevity boom will make us sorry to be alive," *The Atlantic*, May 2005, vol. 295, no.4, p. 94.

# Glossary

**advance health care directive**—Instructions expressing a patient's wishes about medical care in extreme situations and when the patient cannot communicate.

**bioethics**—The study of the ethical implications of medical and biological research and practices.

**clone**—An exact genetic copy of an organism.

**Do-Not-Resuscitate order**—A doctor's order directing medical personnel not to attempt CPR if a patient's heart or lungs fail.

**double effect**—The principle that a medication or treatment may be used under certain conditions (such as to relieve pain) even though it might have unintended negative effects as well.

**euthanasia**—The act of killing someone painlessly, usually to relieve suffering.

**GE foods/GMOs**—Foods that have had genes changed or added to provide a benefit, such as making them more resistant to disease.

**gene therapy**—Treatment of disorders by implanting engineered genes into a patient's cells.

**genetic engineering**—Altering the structure of genes in a living organism.

**genome**—The genetic material of an organism.

**germline therapy**—A treatment that changes the genetic structure of very early embryos so that particular diseases or conditions are eliminated and cannot be handed down to offspring.

**Hayflick limit**—The point at which cells stop dividing further.

**hospice**—A system that provides end-of-life care—medical, psychological, and spiritual—to terminally ill patients and their families.

**Human Genome Project**—A multinational effort to map the human genome.

**in vitro fertilization**—Joining of the sperm and egg in a petri dish to form an embryo, which is then placed in a woman's uterus.

**Nuremburg Code**—A set of ten points of principle regarding human subjects in biological experiments.

**persistent vegetative state (PVS)**—A state of being awake yet unaware, caused by brain damage.

**somatic gene therapy**—Gene therapy that treats a patient but does not pass the changed trait to his or her descendants.

**stem cells**—Cells that have not developed a specific function of their own; they can develop into any of the organs and tissues of the body.

**surrogate mother**—One who bears a child for another, either by becoming pregnant by another woman's partner or by carrying the embryo for another couple.

**triage**—Sorting of medical cases according to seriousness, so that the most urgent for whom there is some hope are cared for first.

**vivisection**—Dissection of a living animal.

# Further Reading

## Books

Espejo, Roman, editor. *Biomedical Ethics.* San Diego: Greenhaven Press, 2002.

Friedlander, Mark P., Jr. *Outbreak: Disease Detectives at Work.* Minneapolis: Lerner Publications, 2000.

Jackson, Linda. *Euthanasia.* Chicago: Raintree, 2005.

Snedden, Robert, *Medical Ethics: Changing Attitudes, 1900–2000.* Austin, Tex.: Raintree Steck-Vaughn, 2000.

Parson, Ann B. *The Proteus Effect: Stem Cells and Their Promise for Medicine.* Washington, D.C.: Joseph Henry Press, 2004.

Toriello, James. *The Human Genome Project.* New York: Rosen, 2003.

Yount, Lisa. *Biotechnology and Genetic Engineering.* New York: Facts on File, 2000.

## Internet Addresses

Medical College of Wisconsin: Center for the Study of Bioethics
**<http://www.mcw.edu/bioethics>**

National Institutes of Health: Bioethics Resources on the Web
**<http://www.nih.gov/sigs/bioethics>**

The President's Council on Bioethics
**<http://www.bioethics.gov>**

# Index